The Negotiated Order
of the School

WILFRED B. W. MARTIN

MACMILLAN OF CANADA
MACLEAN-HUNTER PRESS

ISBN   0-7705-1338-7

This book has been published with the help of a grant from the Social Science Research Council, using funds provided by the Canada Council.

Printed in Canada for
The Macmillan Company of Canada Limited

Contents

371.102
M383

Acknowledgements

Expressions of appreciation are due the teaching staffs and the students of the schools that participated in this study. Despite my frequent intrusions on their valuable time, their co-operation continued throughout the research procedures. I have conformed to tradition in protecting the anonymity of those who participated in this research, by using pseudonyms in referring to them and their schools.

I am deeply indebted to S. Lee Spray of Kent State University, Peter M. Hall of the University of Missouri, and Raymond N. Morris of York University for their consultations during the development of this study and their reading of the early drafts. I owe debts to Nels Anderson of the University of New Brunswick and Robert A. Stebbins of the University of Texas, who willingly endured the task of critically reading the drafts of this manuscript. Valuable comments on various parts of the preliminary manuscript were also made by my colleagues Barbara Pepperdene and Noel Iverson. I am also grateful to T. C. Fairley for editorial assistance; and to Thelma Clarke for typing. Notwithstanding these comments, the author alone is responsible for the shortcomings of this book.

The earlier formulations on the negotiation framework that I presented in articles in *The Sociology of Education* and

The Canadian Review of Sociology and Anthropology are elaborated on in different parts of this book. The permission of these journals to include that material here is appreciated.

A research grant from the University of New Brunswick aided in the secretarial cost of preparing the manuscript. I also wish to thank the Social Science Research Council of Canada. The book has been published with the help of a grant from the Social Science Research Council of Canada, using funds provided by the Canada Council.

Finally, a big vote of appreciation goes to my wife, Eileen, for her understanding and support throughout the project.

WILFRED B. W. MARTIN
University of New Brunswick

Introduction

Social interaction has been the subject of much research and writing, reflecting numerous theoretical orientations. For example, some theorists have viewed interaction as a sort of mechanistic conformity to a role script, while others have used an exchange-theory perspective. Another orientation that has received considerable attention in recent years is that of symbolic interactionism. The conceptual foundations of this orientation are found primarily in pragmatism, the chief lines of development in America extending from William James through Charles Horton Cooley, William I. Thomas and George H. Mead to the many present-day theorists—for example, Herbert Blumer, Anselm Strauss, and Tamotsu Shibutani.

While agreeing with the basic assumptions of the symbolic interactionist approach to social interaction, the author offers a conceptual framework of negotiation that contains specific directives on the way interaction may be systematically observed and analysed from this perspective. The empirical viability of this conceptual framework is demonstrated as it is used to analyse the negotiating of interactive roles and agendas in teacher-pupil and teacher-teacher interactions in both classroom and open-plan-area team-teaching situations.

A certain amount of jargon is inevitable whenever a

sociological orientation is used to analyse social interaction. Such jargon often hampers communication. To reduce this problem I have, in the course of the discussion, elaborated briefly on many of the concepts when they first appear. Some of these concepts have been developed from the present research in the school setting. In such cases, the terms identifying them are presented in italics when first used. These terms are not only defined, but are also exemplified with empirical data from the school setting. Other concepts are explained in footnotes. However, the central importance of certain concepts for an understanding of this study prompts the inclusion here of brief notes on a few of these concepts, to enable the reader to relate more readily to the orientation of the study.

Symbolic interactionism is based on three premises: (a) "Human beings act towards things on the basis of the meanings that the things have for them." (b) These meanings are derived from, or arise "out of, the social interaction that one has with one's fellows". (c) "These meanings are handled in, and modified through, an interpretative process used by the person in dealing with the things he encounters" (Blumer, 1969:2). These premises give rise to concepts such as "definition of the situation", "plans of action", "joint actions", "role-taking", and "role-making".

The definition of the situation is a process whereby an individual gives meaning to a situation into which he enters. It involves him in identifying and interpreting his immediate physical and social environment. He is then led to formulate a plan of action to deal with this environment. In developing and carrying out his plans of action, he is not necessarily following the exact prescription for his particular position in the social situation. On some occasions, there is no exact prescription on how to behave. Even if there is such prescription, the individual is constructing his action and not merely releasing it in response to the situation. It is not merely a stimulus-response set-up, in that a certain amount of thinking occurs before the response is made. The fitting together of the various responses or actions in the situation gives rise to joint actions.

Also, as part of the definition of the situation, an individual attempts to understand how others see him and the interactions he is involved in. That is, he attempts to see the situation by taking the roles of others. However, in the final analysis, an individual acts according to his own definition of the situation, through his interpretations of what he thinks others expect of him. Therefore, it is said that an individual is often involved in role-making. These concepts portray the dynamic aspects of social interaction. Rather than assuming that interaction is the direct result of the rules and regulations that are applied to the situation, it is assumed that interaction is produced through the processes of defining and redefining situations. In other words, to the symbolic interactionist, the individual is regarded as an active occupant of a social identity. His lines of action are fitted together through a process of interpretation. This process is present, to a greater or lesser extent, in all situations, even those that are highly structured.

Waller (1932:311) has pointed out that the social process in teacher-pupil interaction is often flexible and spontaneous. Teachers and pupils work out a definition of the situation together in terms of the needs and desires of all concerned. The social order thus developed is not rigid but continuously changing. It has also been noted that the role of the modern teacher is not " 'given' (in the sense that one steps into assigned duties)", but it "has to be achieved in relation with other teachers. It is a role which is no longer made but has to be made" (Bernstein, 1967). The social processes involved in the developing social order of teacher-pupil and teacher-teacher relations are analysed in detail in this study. Episodes of negotiation in each of these two categories of interaction are presented in detail to show the intricate nature of interactions in teaching situations. The analysis and presentation are centred around five parts of the conceptual framework of negotiations: the existence and expression of ambiguities and disagreements, the power relations, the strategies and stages used by the negotiators, the temporal aspects of negotiation, and the outcomes of the negotiation processes. This kind of analysis brings out the similarities and differences between the processes involved in negotiations in different school settings.

While some kinds of bargain, demonstration, and social-emotional strategy are present in the negotiations in both teacher-pupil and teacher-teacher situations, other strategies used by teachers in negotiating with their colleagues in team situations are different from those they use to negotiate with their pupils. The similarities and differences between the strategies used in various situations are analysed in detail. In addition, both the temporal aspects and the outcomes of negotiations as perceived by the negotiators themselves are analysed. After intensive analyses of both teacher-pupil and teacher-teacher negotiations in various types of schools, the theoretical and empirical boundaries of negotiation are further illuminated by a discussion of the distinctiveness of negotiations, among the interactions that take place in the school.

In the final chapter, the theoretical and practical implications of the findings are given. The intent of this chapter is twofold: first, to add to the development of a theory of the negotiations that take place in formal organizational settings, in general, and the school, in particular; second, to isolate the practical aspects of the findings.

Members of organizations of all kinds, but especially of the school organization, will, it is hoped, find insights here into their interactions with each other, and help in identifying aspects of these interactions that they may want deliberately to continue or discontinue. In addition, the author hopes that the weaknesses in the conceptual framework and analysis given here will suggest research issues for fellow analysts on the processes involved in social interaction.

THE NEGOTIATED ORDER OF THE SCHOOL

1

The Negotiation Framework

All social interactions lie somewhere on a continuum ranging from conformity to individualism. Social scientists' approaches to interaction may be placed on a similar continuum. For example, some have seen role performance as a mechanistic conformity to a role script. The implication is that the lines of action, even the gestures, of each actor are specified. This perspective is based on the assumption that a role is a set of expectations towards the holders of a particular social position or status.[1] Much of the research on the formation of group norms is based on such an assumption. This is demonstrated by the fact that the issues of individual conformity and change, as well as the issue of group pressures on the deviant, have inspired the core of the literature on the formation of norms and social control in the small group (Hare, 1964:218). A completely different perspective of role has been developed by Turner (1962). He has pointed out that an individual often frames his behaviour as if roles had "unequivocal existence and clarity", while in fact they " 'exist' with varying degrees of concreteness and consistency"; consequently, the process of "role-making" comes into existence (Turner, 1962:22). Turner also sees role-taking as a process rather than as an act of conformity to formalized role prescriptions.

Homans (1958: 1961) and Blau (1964) have analysed social interaction from an exchange-theory point of view. They allow for the emergence of relationships through interactions, but they emphasize the patterned end product of these interactions. This emphasis is also followed by Nord (1969) in his demonstration of the value of social exchange theory for bringing together what is known about conformity and social approval.[2]

Another, but not completely different, approach to the analysis of social interaction has been presented by symbolic interactionists.[3] Blumer's (1969:78-89) presentation of "society as symbolic interaction" isolates the essential features of this perspective as given by G. H. Mead. These features presuppose

that human society is made up of individuals who have selves (that is, make indications to themselves); that individual action is a construction and not a release, being built up by the individual through noting and interpreting features of the situations in which he acts; that group or collective action consists of the aligning of individual actions, brought about by the individuals' interpreting or taking into account each other's actions. [Blumer, 1969:82]

Blumer also states:

From the standpoint of symbolic interaction, social organization is a framework inside of which acting units develop their actions. Structural features such as "culture", "social systems", "social stratification", or "social roles" set conditions for their action but do not determine their action. People—that is, acting units—do not act toward culture, social structure or the like; they act toward situations. Social organization enters into action only to the extent to which it shapes situations in which people act, and to the extent to which it supplies fixed sets of symbols which people use in interpreting their situations. [Blumer, 1969:87-8]

Although social interaction has been a subject of much theorizing and empirical research from a variety of perspectives, understanding the processes it involves still presents an imposing problem. The position adopted here is that the theoretical orientation of symbolic interactionism can contribute to our understanding of the social interactions representing different points on the conformity-individualism continuum.

However, directives are needed for the use of this orientation to observe and analyse social interactions. In attempting to fulfil this need, this chapter will outline a conceptual framework of negotiation within the general theoretical orientation of symbolic interactionism.[4] Before such a framework is presented, the sociology of negotiation will be discussed. This discussion and the discussion of a conceptual framework of negotiation, together with the presentation in the next chapter on the school from an interactionist perspective, will provide the necessary background for the research reported on. Specifically, the purposes of the research were (a) to test the empirical viability of a conceptual framework of negotiation, (b) to analyse teacher-pupil and teacher-teacher negotiations that take place in closed- and open-plan schools, and (c) to move towards the development of a substantive theory of informal negotiations, in the school in particular, and in formal organizations in general.

THE SOCIOLOGY OF NEGOTIATION

The literature that addresses itself to negotiation may be subsumed under two categories, one of which deals with the negotiations of representatives of two or more parties "who are in direct interaction for the purpose of obtaining mutually acceptable resolutions of one or more problems about which the parties disagree" (McGrath, 1966:109); this is the union-management category of negotiations. The second category covers the negotiations that take place in the social interactions of everyday life. This study focuses on the second category of negotiations.

On a theoretical level, Erving Goffman has been concerned with the processes involved in negotiating various aspects of social interaction. He (Goffman, 1959:106-40) argues, for example, that interactants operate between a "back region" and a "front region". Performances are planned in the former and performed in the latter. We take "role distance" in certain degrading circumstances (Goffman, 1961:85-152). That is to say, we step outside the expectations of a role when we view the performance of these expectations as degrading to our self-conception. In a later work, Goffman (1970) analyses further the deceptions, conflicts, and negotiations in the routines of human conduct. He adds to the exchange-theory approach to social interaction by noting that individuals not only calculate their interactions but also attempt to manage them. While Goffman is concerned with negotiations, he frequently emphasizes the stable aspects in interaction and demonstrates how people must work at keeping their relations stable.[5]

Informal negotiation between individuals attempting to arrive at a common understanding of specific issues has been demonstrated to exist in a variety of social settings in everyday life. For example, Roth's (1962; 1963:1-62) analysis of timetables of patients and physicians vividly demonstrates the existence of negotiation in hospitals for the treatment of tuberculosis. He states:

> The desire of patients to cut short their hospitalization often leads them to try to make a deal with the physician to alter treatment timetables. . . . [Physicians] often become quite angry with patients who assail them with arguments, threats, name calling, and (in the case of women) tears in an effort to get their conferences, passes, and discharges sooner than the physicians want to give them. . . .
> Such pressure from the patients is successful in the sense that it often does get patients results that they want sooner than they would get them by simply sitting back and waiting. . . . Every physician does give in to pressure from patients at some time or other. The job of the patients is simply to find the physician's breaking point or weak spot. [Roth, 1963:48-9]

Roth refers to these interactions as bargaining processes. He relates these processes both to the nature of the hospital structure and to the organizational positions of the actors within it. He shows how these interactions are simultaneously patterned and affected by the social structure of the hospital, and yet their outcomes are uncertain because of the conflicts that arise and because the physicians do, in fact, compromise with their patients.

Balint (1957), an English psychoanalyst, gives examples of how the psychoanalyst and the patient negotiate. He notes that a psychoanalyst may reject the reasons a patient gives for coming to him and offer counter-proposals until an "illness" acceptable to both parties is found. Evidence indicates that many criminal convictions are decided on through a process referred to as "bargain justice" (Newman, 1966). Newman claims that a bargain is often struck with the prosecutor; the prosecutor will reduce the charge if a plea of guilty is made. This procedure is so common that space is frequently provided for the defendant, his lawyer, and a representative of the prosecutor's office to meet and "negotiate the plea".

A model of negotiation in studying hospitals for the treatment of mental illness was used by Strauss *et al.* (1963; 1964). Schatzman and Bucher's (1964) examination of the ways psychiatric professionals negotiate the tasks they perform (that is, how they develop an institutional order) resulted from the same fieldwork. Bucher and Stelling (1969) elaborated on the model of negotiation by further developing the argument that bureaucratic theory is of limited value in the analysis of professional organizations. They demonstrated also that professional organizations may be better understood by the use of a language of political process that emphasizes negotiation and shifting alliances. Strauss *et al.* (1964:377) suggest that the "arena-negotiation model" has utility beyond the analysis of formal organizations. Following up this idea, P. M. Hall (1972) has shown that this model may be useful for describing the nature of social relations in society and for providing insights into the conduct of national and international politics.

The concern with negotiation in this study is centred on a basic Meadian problem in day-to-day social interactions. This is not the same as the problem of maintaining a given social order. Instead, it is a problem of accommodating methods of change that are in the order of social interaction itself.[6] This concern means that the focus here is on the negotiations between parties who are engaged in co-ordination, joint planning, and so on. The parties are not formal representatives of different groups interacting for the sole purpose of reaching acceptable resolutions of problems. Rather, the parties are involved in day-to-day interactions that have become problematic, and they must reach an agreement so that they may proceed with the business at hand. These negotiations are informal in that they refer to processes in which two or more actors attempt to reach a collective agreement over their mutual interactions or their joint interactions with a third party during day-to-day interactions.

"To bargain" and "to negotiate" have similar meanings. To bargain has been defined as meaning: "to discuss or haggle over terms for selling or buying" (Funk and Wagnalls, 1965:114). To negotiate is "to treat or bargain with others in order to reach an agreement" (Funk and Wagnalls, 1965:849). Sociologists and social psychologists often use these verbs interchangeably to describe the exchange of social objects and the processes of offering counter-proposals and reaching compromises in a variety of settings. In this study, they are used to refer to different but often intricately interrelated processes. *Bargaining* is the process whereby different social objects—tangible and non-tangible—are exchanged at a cost that is considered by at least one of the parties involved to be favourable. Each party in the interaction wants an object that the other party can provide.[7] The parties involved in bargaining have complementary, sometimes antagonistic, interests. In contrast, *negotiating* is more inclusive; it refers to the total set of processes whereby actors in pursuit of common interests try to arrive at a settlement or arrangement with each other or with a third party. Negotiation, as such, may involve implicit or explicit bargaining, as well as other interaction tactics.

The common feature of bargains and negotiations is that they are oriented towards a coming-to-terms. Their distinctiveness lies in the fact that a bargain is only an exchange, while a negotiation often includes a variety of interaction strategies including bargains. And while bargains may centre on unshared interests, in that neither party is concerned with what the other does with the objects once they have been exchanged, negotiations are always centred on shared interests, in that both parties have vested interests in their overall interactions and these interests are salient in the processes of coming to terms. For example, a teacher and his pupils may make an exchange concerning the noise level in a teaching situation and the assigning of detentions. The teacher offers not to give the pupils detentions if the noise level is reduced to a level acceptable to him. The pupils, by their subsequent actions, agree to this exchange. Neither the teacher nor the pupils experienced any ambiguity or disagreement when the offer was made. The offer was acceptable to both sides, and it was considered favourable, at least by the teacher. Also, the teacher and pupils had unshared interests, in that the teacher wanted the noise level reduced and the pupils did not want to have to serve detentions. Since these characteristics were present, the interaction may be classified as a bargaining sequence. However, such offers do not always result in an immediate bargain. They may produce episodes of negotiation. If one of the actors does not accept the offer of the other or there is some experienced ambiguity in the situation, and if they have a shared salient interest other than that of reaching an agreement on the objects being exchanged, they will negotiate over the disagreement or ambiguity.

When defined in this way, negotiation encompasses some of the research on the bargaining process. Miller's (1970) analysis of the bargains between medical students and faculty, Freidson's (1961) and Roth's (1962; 1963) view of doctor-patient bargaining, and Browne's (1973) discussion of "a sociology of the bargain" in her analysis of "the used car game" pin-point some of the processes of negotiating in social interactions. Similarly, research by some experimental psychologists in isolating and describing the bargaining situation may be described as research on the processes of negotiation, because strategies other than bargains are used in the interaction.[8]

Negotiation may take place during any phase of an interaction process, that is, during the negotiation of social identities, interactive roles, agendas, or life courses (McCall and Simmons, 1966: *passim*). In some situations, all four of these phases may be negotiated simultaneously and they may be so intertwined that empirical separation is impossible. Other situations may preclude negotiating on one or more of them.

Social identities. Negotiations at the social identity level involve the establishment of agreements on specific aspects in the broad outline of who each party is in terms of social categories—for example, teacher, wife, student, and so on. It is a way of settling which, how many, and how much of a person's salient role identities will be incorporated into his performance.[9] The social bargaining model of Weinstein and Deutschberger (1964) implies that a person must have an image of the identity of those with whom he is interacting as well as establish his own identity. Foote (1951:18) has noted that the "establishment of one's own identity to oneself is as important in interaction as to establish it for the others. One's own identity in a situation is not absolutely given but is more or less problematic." Goffman (1961:7-81) has claimed that once an agreement between two or more individuals or groups is reached the rules of relevance and irrelevance are set and must be treated with utmost respect if the entire encounter is not to be threatened. However, Strauss (1959:44-88) has pointed out that once the definition of the situation is upset a new agreement may be negotiated. Having reached an agreement on the aspects of the social identities to be honoured in a particular social situation, as well as on a broad outline of the rules to be followed in the encounter, the actors are free to negotiate their interactive roles.

Interactive roles. Interactive roles are the actual role performances of the actors in the situation. McCall and Simmons (1966:67) state:

> The interactive role is a plausible line of action characteristic and expressive of the particular personality that happens to occupy the given position and represents that person's mode of coming to grips with the general expectations held toward someone in his position.

The actors' role identities and expectations are involved in the negotiating of their interactive roles. The simultaneous processes of expressing an image of the other and presenting oneself may also be intricately related to this negotiating. In certain situations these processes may involve illegitimate tactics.[10] To reiterate, interactive roles involve complex social processes. It is not merely a matter of conformity to an unequivocal set of expectations.

Agendas. Agendas refer to the schedules of performances that become necessary when a single performance cannot satisfy individuals' needs or desires. In situations where there is an allotted time in which individuals must interact in some way (for example, in the teacher-pupil situation), the setting up of agendas may become an important part of the interaction process. In all situations, the agendas are, to some extent, negotiated, and this rarely occurs with equal voice by both actors.

Life courses. It is important to note that the activities one chooses for a particular situation automatically make some other courses of action impossible. Also, each individual has only a finite store of time and resources. Therefore, he must "juggle the multitudinous commitments and demands of his positions and relationships and the demands following from his role identity hierarchies in such a way as to negotiate a 'safe' and 'meaningful' passage through life" (McCall and Simmons, 1966:234). Life courses are negotiated, and the negotiation takes place within the boundaries of the various elements that are, more or less, salient in the situation.

In all phases of social interaction (that is, in the mapping out of social identities, interactive roles, agendas, and life courses) individuals act towards situations. The situations, and the symbols people use in interpreting them, are, to some extent, shaped by structural features. In order to investigate simultaneously the processes whereby individuals act in social situations and the extent to which structural variables determine the situation and thereby influence the experiences of the actors and the interpersonal relations among them, this study has used aspects of the models of negotiation, as described above, and aspects of role theory. Models of negotiation were introduced by Roth, McCall and Simmons, Strauss, and others as alternatives to the conception of mechanistic conformity to a role script in studying social interaction and analysing social organizations. Neither the idea that everything is negotiable nor the idea that interlocking roles are set by status within a social organization is adequate to describe the dynamics of interactions that take place in ordinary daily living.[11] Instead of adopting either one of these approaches, this study suggests that a combination of some aspects of each would prove a worthwhile approach to the study of social interactions. Hence, the following is offered as a conceptual framework for focusing on the negotiated aspects of interactions in everyday life.

A CONCEPTUAL FRAMEWORK OF NEGOTIATION

Negotiation as a conceptual framework has five major parts. These are (a) preconditions, (b) extent, (c) stages, (d) strategies, and (e) outcomes of the negotiation processes.

Preconditions. The preconditions that have to be met before a set of relations may be said to be part of an episode of negotiation may be outlined as follows: (a) At least two actors are involved. (b) At least one of the actors perceives the situation concerning interactive roles and/or agendas in at least one of the following ways: (i) as a new situation in which there is either ambiguity concerning guidelines or a disagreement, or (ii) as a recurrent situation in which there is either ambiguity because different results have occurred for similar situations or a disagreement.[12] (c) Given the existence of an ambiguity and/or a disagreement, one or more of the following conditions must also be present: (i) no one in the interaction has sufficient power to realize his aims,[13] (ii) if one or more of the actors has the power to realize his aims, he is reluctant to use it, (iii) the negotiators are reluctant to abandon the situation. This reluctance occurs because the costs of the situation are seen as less than the rewards that might be attained by continued interactions within the group. The factors that may result in the situation being perceived in this way include contractual and voluntary commitments, attachment to all or some aspects of the group and/or the organization in which the situation takes place, career plans, and viewing the situation as the only one in which it is possible to achieve one's aims. (d) At least one of the actors hopes to achieve a goal in the situation—a goal that is achievable at the moment only through negotiation.

Extent. Negotiation will, undoubtedly, be more prevalent in some situations than in others. The extent of negotiation may be analysed by considering each of the following: (a) the content of negotiation, that is, the issues around which the interactive roles and/or agendas are negotiated; (b) the direction of negotiation (in seeking out the direction of negotiation the idea is to see who influences whom and, conversely, who is influenced by whom); and (c) the intensity of negotiation, that is, the extent to which changes take place over a particular period of time as a result of the negotiation, or the extent to which decisions made during the negotiation processes are implemented.

Stages. First of all, it should be noted that the idea of stages of negotiation as analysed here is not the same as the idea that occurs in earlier writings on the stages and phases of group development.[14] This study does not attempt to analyse or even isolate any of the transformation or evolutionary processes *per se* of the groups observed. Instead, it focuses on the processes involved in coming to terms over the disagreements and ambiguities that are experienced by one or more of the actors within the groups. With this frame of reference, a stage may be defined as a set of social acts that are demarcated by their nature or time sequence, and that are enacted as parts of the over-all processes of the interactions that occur when individuals attempt to achieve specific outcomes. Different stages may require different spans of time, from a few moments to several hours, days, or even weeks. While the boundaries of the stages of negotiation are often difficult to determine, they frequently include conspicuous units of interaction. For example, the stage of communicating one's goals for the interaction, and the stages of defining and redefining the situation, may be empirically inseparable, either in their nature of interaction or in their time sequence. On the other hand, the stage of communicating one's goals for the interaction will obviously be a different stage from that of solemnizing an agreement that has been reached on a negotiated issue. Even though it is doubtful that the stages of negotiation will have a neat or regular order, they will undoubtedly include some of the following: (a) communicating goals of the interaction, (b) defining and redefining the situation, (c) attempting to put alter on the defensive by drawing his attention to new materials and/or using other persuasive tactics, (d) displaying one's bargaining counters and evaluating those of others, (e) re-evaluating alter's position to see whether what has been done thus far has achieved the desired ends, (f) going through these stages again, (g) reaching a working agreement concerning the issue(s) negotiated, and (h) solemnizing the agreement.

Strategies. Strategies are activities designed to influence an individual or group to act in a way that accords with one's goals. They may involve various forms of impression management (Goffman, 1959), ingratiation (Jones, 1964), and other forms of strategic interaction (Goffman, 1970) including both genuine and fraudulent expressions of affect and solidarity. The various forms of expression may be important for agreements that are not part of the more institutionalized patterns of interaction, but are accepted as legitimate by the actors in the situation. In fact, this type of agreement is frequently the goal or an important part of the goal of negotiation. Also, while stages of negotiation are not strategies *per se*, one can, as a matter of strategy, try to change the focus from one stage to the next. It may also be a strategy to overlook certain stages (for example, the implementation stage), so that the agreements are prevented from being binding.

Outcomes. There are at least three possible outcomes to the negotiation that takes place in a given situation. Two assume a zero sum game, while the third does not.[15] It may be that a compromise is met; that is, a give-and-take situation exists. A multitude of different combinations could occur here, ranging from each giving and taking an equal amount to the opposite situation in which one side is almost completely overpowered by the other. Secondly, it is theoretically possible that one of the actors will not compromise at all. His decision is carried out at the expense of the others, who are seen by some objective measure as losing ground. However, even under the most rigid circumstances and given an unequal distribution of power, some compromise may be necessary. Thirdly, winning, or refusing to compromise, does not always have a strictly competitive implication. It does not always imply a zero sum game; that is, it does not mean that one person can win only if another loses. In such cases, it is not winning relative to others one may not want to offend. Instead, it means gaining relative to one's own value system or relative to a third party who is not present.

Before the negotiation framework is used to analyse the interactions in the school, it will be appropriate to give an overview of these interactions from an interactionist perspective and to elaborate on the elements of the negotiation framework with reference to the analysis of specific social interactions in a school setting. This will be done in the next chapter.

1. See, for example, Parsons (1951), Merton (1957; especially chapter 9), and Gross, Mason, and McEachern (1958).
2. Exchange theory borrows heavily from economics. Briefly, the main idea is that we are always calculating our costs and rewards from our interactions, with the aim of maximizing the rewards to ourselves. The academic development of exchange theory together with an analysis of its present explanatory power, with particular reference to the findings in laboratory settings, have been presented in a concise form by Gergen (1969).
3. While exchange and symbolic interactionism are, in some aspects, separate theoretical orientations, they have certain points of convergence. Four of these are discussed by Singlemann (1972).
4. In addition to Blumer's (1969) presentation on symbolic interactionism, statements on this perspective are given by Rose (1962; especially pages 3-19), Shibutani (1961), and P. M. Hall (1972). A textbook by Lindesmith and Strauss (1968) also exemplifies this orientation.
5. See, for example, Goffman's (1967:5-45) paper "On Face-Work".
6. Mead (1934; 1936) has argued that the problem of society is centred round the relationship between change and order. "How can you present order and structure in society and yet bring about the changes that need to take place, are taking place? How can you bring those changes about in orderly fashion and yet preserve order? To bring about change is seemingly to destroy the given order, and yet society does and must change. That is the problem, to incorporate the methods of change into the order of society itself " (Mead, 1936:360-1).
7. If a party outside of a particular bargaining process can grant the desired reward(s) to one or both of the actors within it, then the actor(s) concerned may attempt to bargain with this outside party with the intention of selecting the situation that benefits him (them) most.
8. See, for example, Deutsch (1958), Deutsch and Krauss (1960; 1962); Borah (1963), Gallo (1966), and Brown (1968).
9. Role identity is an imaginary view that a person has of himself. It

includes both the idealized concept a person may have of himself as the occupant of a particular social identity, and the person's concept of how he should act in that role (McCall and Simmons, 1966: 67-71; 86-7). A terse discussion of the terms "identity" and "the negotiation of identity" may be found in Brittan (1973:147-65).

10. By systematically presenting the forms, guises, and antecedents of ingratiation as well as its implications for social relations, Jones (1964) has illuminated the illegitimate tactics that may be involved in these processes.

11. Several writers have offered both theoretical statements and empirical demonstrations of the validity of this statement with respect to the school organization (for example, Waller, 1932:279-317; Corwin, 1965:301-40; Geer, 1968; Jackson, 1968; Martin, 1970a; Stebbins, 1971).

12. All of the situations listed here as being new or recurrent may, at some time or other, conduce to "role creation". Role creation and negotiation "are two sides of the same order, when one is present so is the other" (Bucher and Stelling, 1969:5). The idea is that when a person is carving out his role performances he is simultaneously negotiating with his counter-identities; hence, interactive roles are being negotiated. One's counter-identities may not experience ambiguity or disagreement, at least not at the beginning of the negotiation.

13. Some of the problems in defining social power have been isolated by Wrong (1969). In this analysis, "power" is used to refer to the intended production of a desired effect on another person. There are a number of reasons why power may exist. These include such things as reward, punishment, legal authority, identification, and expertise (French and Raven, 1958; 1959).

14. See, for example, Bennis and Shepard (1961), Mills (1964), and Slater (1966).

15. A zero sum game is a situation in which one person wins what another person loses. Conversely, what one loses the other wins. Hence, the wins and losses add up to zero.

2

An Interactionist Perspective
of the School

The dominant themes in the literature on the school centre round administrative procedures and classroom instruction. Many aspects of social interactions in the school have been largely ignored or underemphasized, for example, the processes involved in teacher-teacher and teacher-pupil interactions.[1] This study focuses on the processes involved in these social interactions. As a preliminary to this discussion, the following key terms will be defined: "open-plan school", "closed-plan school", "mixed-plan school", and "team teaching".

An open-plan school is a school that combines the organization of an open environment for learning with open physical areas. Each open-plan school may include several such areas. These areas are architecturally open and each has a team of teachers working with a group of pupils.[2] A closed-plan school does not have architectural openness. It is a traditional type of school with classrooms and only one teacher and usually only one grade level in each classroom. Even when team teaching is done in this type of school there is usually only one teacher in each classroom at any one time during regular teaching sessions. When a school has both open- and closed-plan areas it will be referred to here as a mixed-plan school. If a teaching team is using both classrooms and open areas, this physical area of the school will be referred to as a mixed-plan area. In fact, a mixed-plan area has either flexible walls to permit variation of the space used for team teaching, or permanent walls so arranged that at least one classroom and one open area may be used simultaneously.

The literature of education contains a plethora of definitions of team teaching. Here are two that are stated in broad terms:

> ... an arrangement whereby two or more teachers, with or without teacher aides, co-operatively plan, instruct and evaluate one or more class groups in an appropriate instructional space and given length of time, so as to take advantage of the special competencies of the team members. [Trump and Baynhan, 1963:3]

> ... a type of instructional organization, involving teaching personnel and the students assigned to them, in which two or more teachers are given responsibility, working together for all or a significant part of the instruction of the same group of students. [Shaplin and Olds, 1964:15]

Despite the many varieties and applications of the basic principles of team teaching, this concept refers, essentially, from an interactionist perspective, to a type of staff use that involves co-operative planning and striving for a working consensus through more or less unrestrained communication. Therefore, "team teaching" in this study denotes two or more teachers who share the responsibilities and functions of instructing a group of pupils in one or more subject areas, for example, mathematics, social studies, general science. It is assumed that sharing requires at least some interacting before a working agreement is reached on matters of common concern, such as planning, evaluating, and pupil activities.

ORGANIZATIONAL SETTING AND
TEACHERS' DEFINITION OF THE SITUATION

Mass education requires teachers and pupils to submit to some sort of formal organization. How strongly this organization resembles a bureaucracy varies between school systems, and even between schools within the same system. The way educators have adopted bureaucratic models from other settings has been documented by Callahan (1962). Dreeben

(1970:77) has noted that the bureaucratic model provides rough guidelines for understanding the relations of authority within the school when it is applied to the administrative component and to the teachers, but is of little use for understanding the situations in which teachers and pupils come together for instructional purposes. Following a similar line of argument, Roberts (1971:310-53) claims that the adoption of bureaucratic methods of control in the school, in teacher-teacher and teacher-pupil interactions, may produce among the pupils widespread hostility and apathy, and a rejection of the goals of the organization. How greatly the formal organizational structure affects the processes of interactions will usually vary somewhat from one school to another. Teachers' definitions of situations in the school will indicate, to some extent, the effect of the formal organization on their interactions with each other and with their pupils.[3]

Before meaningful action can take place, the participants in any social situation must evaluate it in terms of their action orientations and the action orientations of others as they are seen to affect the situation. From a generally accepted educational viewpoint, the principal action orientations of teachers and pupils, both in classroom and in open-plan areas, are teaching and learning, respectively. The theoretically ideal team-teaching situation exists when teachers "find an optimum use of technology, co-operatively instruct a group of students, varying the size of the student groups and procedures with the purpose of instruction, and spending staff time and energy in ways that will make the best use of their respective competencies" (Beggs, 1964:76). However, during the enactment of behaviour in particular social situations, the ideal of completely matched perspectives and goals is seldom present. The teacher and his pupils may have principal action orientations that are, for various reasons, at variance. In addition, their secondary action orientations may be at a considerable distance from each other. Even when the goals of two parties are the same, complete agreement on how to attain them in a particular situation may be difficult to achieve.

We will now turn to a discussion of the definition of the situation with reference to the teacher-pupil and teacher-

teacher interactions in team-teaching situations in open-plan and closed-plan schools.

Teacher-Pupil Interaction

Theoretically, the definition of the situation, even in the most routinized and mechanized teaching situation, may require relatively complicated techniques (Stebbins, 1971).[4] In highly regimented teaching situations it is a definition in terms of a relatively rigid social order and teacher domination of all social life. This is a domination that attempts to leave nothing to improvisation. The following remarks by teachers in traditionally organized inner-city schools demonstrate the teachers' desire to control all of the situations in their classrooms and to allow only a minimum of negotiation between themselves and their pupils:

The best thing that happened to me the first day was being such a tyrant and not showing that I was a softie right away. I figured while I was sitting there that the children were probably hating me but I wasn't taking it to heart because I wanted to get them straight right away on what I expected of them and not let them take advantage of me. [Fuchs, 1969:9]

When I speak to you, you do as I say! I am the teacher here! I am in charge! Now get to your room! [Fuchs, 1969:49]

Becker (1952) has reported that there are variations in teacher-pupil relationships along social-class lines. But even in schools where rigid rules exist, the pupils may still exert a subtle and profound influence on the teachers' definition of the situation. In his discussion of the definition of the situation, Waller (1932:292-337) noted the differences between the interaction processes of the "old style" and those of the "newer order of school discipline". Ideally, in the old-style school, the teacher defines the situation in terms of a rigid social order dominated by him, in which the pupils' definition of the situation is irrelevant. In the classroom situation this did not happen. Instead, "pupils inevitably attempted to establish their own social order independently of teachers, and a lethal conflict sprang up between the teacher-directed social process and the social process which students pushed forward." Also, "the social order which the teacher worked out in advance and attempted to establish could never be quite complete" (Waller, 1932:309). Teachers were forced to accept a newer sort of school discipline that included more flexible and spontaneous social processes. It should be noted that the newer social order Waller speaks of is related to, but not to be confused with, the newer type of social order as it exists where open education is being implemented today. For Waller, the newer social order is simply a relaxing of the authoritarian "rod-swinging method of discipline". Today's newer order in teaching situations includes a further relaxation of discipline. Both of these social orders call for a "working out by teacher and students together of a definition of the situation in terms of the needs and desires of all concerned" (Waller, 1932:311). No rigid social order is produced in teacher-pupil interactions, not even in situations where the rod-swinging method of discipline is employed. Both teachers and pupils are continually defining and redefining situations. As the interactions proceed, each actor is required to take others' lines of action into account in devising his own plans. Because of this, the actors are seldom permitted to perform exactly as they would like to. Nor do they conform exactly to the role projected upon them by the other. When a working consensus is reached, it is not characterized by total agreement but rather by an absence of extensive disagreement.[5]

On occasion, teachers are unable to eliminate gross conflicts between themselves and certain of their pupils. As a consequence of failing to negotiate with their pupils, teachers have frequently had to leave some problems unsolved in the course of their attempts to develop and maintain what they see as a satisfactory social order in teaching situations. The solution to these problems comes only when the interaction between the parties concerned is terminated. Fuchs (1969:18) gives an example of a teacher who was "forced" to go to the principal and have a pupil removed from her class. The teacher said: "It's either him or me. I won't continue this way any more." Sometimes a principal will act as an arbitrator between a teacher and a pupil, to avoid having the teacher terminate his interactions with a pupil he has labelled a discipline problem. Remarks by an elementary-school teacher concerning her dealings with a certain pupil and with her principal serve to demonstrate this:

I was getting fed up with Bill's behaviour. He has been misbehaving occasionally all year. Last week he was so bad I drove him out of the classroom and told him I wasn't going to have him back any more. . . . If it wasn't for Mr. Black [the principal] I would not have taken him back. Mr. Black did not want to send him to another classroom because he said that I could handle him better than anyone else. . . . Our principal is really a nice person to work with. . . . Someone has got to have Bill in her classroom. What can the principal really do about it? Anyhow, I took Bill back and he has been pretty good ever since.

Apparently the principal's praise of the teacher's ability "to handle [Bill] better than anyone", together with the high esteem the teacher had for the principal, resulted in her accepting Bill back in her classroom.

The actions of both teachers and pupils in many closed-plan schools are more flexible and spontaneous than is often supposed. The pupils' definitions of situations are frequently taken into consideration by teachers when a social order is being worked out. The open-plan school is characterized, at least theoretically, by dynamic social interactions—more so than the closed-plan school. The dynamic interactions are theoretically possible because of the greater number of pupils and teachers simultaneously visible to each other in the open-plan school. Also, the extended physical and social boundaries of the teaching situations in open-plan schools may be accompanied by an extension in the scope and range of activities that are available to both teachers and pupils. But in both closed- and open-plan areas there are, to a greater or lesser degree, situations that are continually being defined and redefined in terms of the attitudes and interests of the individuals and groups concerned. The development of a working consensus in these situations requires complicated techniques for defining situations and negotiating over interactive roles and agendas.

Teacher-Teacher Interaction

Teachers in schools without team teaching spend most of

their time working as individuals at tasks for which they have sole responsibility. These tasks are not broken down into components and later synthesized through co-ordinated efforts to the extent that this is necessary in team-teaching situations. If team teaching of one kind or another does not exist in a school, the teachers will for the most part be restricted in their informal interactions to activities not directly related to their teaching roles, and to at best very general discussion of the activities and problems of their teaching roles. When team teaching is introduced, the teachers' activities and interactions among themselves take on new dimensions. This discussion is confined to observations of teacher-teacher interaction in team-teaching situations.

Lortie (1964) has argued that teaching teams are likely to take one of two organizational forms: "vertical-bureaucratic" or "horizontal-collegial". In the first, the team leader is a part of the administrative hierarchy of the school, and so, the leader controls and co-ordinates the actions of the other teachers on the team. The second is said to exist when team members are part of a relatively egalitarian, self-regulating instructional group. Regardless of the form of a team, before meaningful action can take place the participants must, to some extent, evaluate each social situation in terms of their principal and subsidiary action orientations.

When teachers plan together, which is one of the essential ingredients of team teaching, new interactive roles and agendas may appear while others are being sustained. In addition to the interactions of teachers at formal meetings and during informal meetings in corridors and staffrooms, open- and mixed-plan teaching set-ups add another dimension to teacher-teacher interaction: the presence of other teachers in the same physical area where one is teaching a lesson or carrying out other activities associated with the teaching process. The fact that teachers can see and often hear each other and that they are in the presence of a greater number of pupils than is found in the classroom during any individual teaching situation must, in some measure, influence both teacher-teacher and teacher-pupil negotiations. The placing together of teachers who are used to a fair measure of authority and

autonomy in the classroom may upset the whole social structure based on the interactions that have hitherto taken place
in the school.

In all types of school, teachers and pupils are able, at least
under certain conditions and to a certain extent, to make
their roles and to act extemporaneously. Also, because there
are numerous ways to behave in team-teaching situations,
especially in open- and mixed-plan school designs, teachers
must be willing to try different approaches. A superintendent
with some teaching experience in an open-plan area gives this
advice to teachers who find themselves in an open-plan school
for the first time:

Don't expect too much too quickly. Both you and the children need
to adapt to the new environment. Be willing to try, admit it didn't
work and plan another approach. Be willing to learn from others.
The open area will expose you to learning from other teachers and
they, in turn, will learn from you. [Ingalls, 1969:6]

Some teachers who have taught both in team-teaching and
in other organizational set-ups have realized that the need for
communication among teachers is greater in team organizations than in other kinds. Team teaching calls forth different
definitions of situations than are necessary in traditionally
organized, non-team-teaching arrangements. One teacher
has helped to clarify this point by analysing the problems
some teachers experienced in moving from a non-team to a
team organization:

The willingness to co-operate and compromise—so necessary in successful team teaching—was a little difficult to learn. Probably as a
carry-over from our days in the single classroom. Our major initial
problems arose from thinking in terms of "mine" rather than "ours"
and "I" rather than "we". [Goss, 1965:82]

Even though the team organizations in closed-plan schools
call for co-operative teacher planning, decision-making, and
evaluating, the fact remains that, as a rule, only one teacher is
in a classroom during the teaching process. Consequently, the
nature and extent of the team co-operation and compromise
that takes place among the teachers will be different in closed
plans than it is in open plans. One teacher offered this observation on team teaching in open-plan schools:

The open-plan idea has given the students the opportunity to become individuals while at the same time it has forced the teachers to work as a team. The teachers could be individuals in the classroom while the students were often forced to do things. The students couldn't make very much choice. Now it is almost the opposite to that situation.

Educators have stressed the need for planning by both the teacher and the school board if team teaching is to be success-ful. Some claim that planning among teachers is best done when they "have similar philosophies in program, housekeep-ing, and discipline" (D. C. Anderson, 1970:6). If this is so, there is a need for careful screening, selection, and assign-ment of teaching personnel. A realization of the need for har-mony is often seen in the criteria used to select teachers for a team. Careful selection can help to control the composition of teaching teams, but even with the most rigid screening processes some differences are bound to arise between teach-ers. These differences may arise simply because there are many issues to be negotiated, resulting in a dynamic interac-tive process of decision-making within the teaching team and between it and the pupils. Sometimes, however, com-munications break down, even among members of a team that was thought to be a relatively homogenous in teaching philosophy and in attitudes about housekeeping and dis-cipline. For example, during the initial phase of this study, the members of a team that the school administration at one time thought to be homogeneous were observed performing as if they were not members of a team. They did not consider or try to accommodate each other's views and activities before initiating their own lines of action. A teacher on this team remarked that the way the members of her team were operat-ing did not make sense. She added that her team had come to the point where it could not "make decisions on the simplest things". This state of affairs was attributed to the teachers' failure to adjust to the physical and social conditions of the open-plan area, although they had all had similar expecta-tions of what should happen in such an area. Of course, the teachers' failure in their new environments was actually a symptom of not getting along together, not a causal explana-tion of it.

Many teachers appear to have overcome any aversion they may have had to losing the authority and autonomy they had when they were not members of a team-teaching organization. They have found ways of defining situations and of communicating these definitions so that they can work together co-operatively. For example, one teacher claimed:

We [the teaching team] had a lot of problems at first. We were miles apart. . . . Of course, we still are in many respects. Then, we feared what would happen if our decisions didn't get accepted, but now we understand each other better.

ELEMENTS OF NEGOTIATION AND INTERACTIONS IN THE SCHOOL

The elements of the negotiation framework will be elaborated on next, with specific reference to teacher-pupil and teacher-teacher interactions. First of all, it should be noted that we are operating here on both subjective and objective levels of analysis, the subjective level being the teachers' and pupils' interpretations of their interactions in situations in which ambiguity and/or disagreement are experienced. However, teachers did not always see as negotiation, episodes of interaction that met the preconditions of negotiation as given in the conceptual framework presented above. In calling these interactions negotiations, the analysis moved to an objective level. This procedure is objective in that the interactions are approached in a way not directly connected with the personal viewpoints of the teachers. Similarly, the elements of the framework were often categorized on an objective level of analysis. Before discussion of the substantive issues of this study, it is appropriate to point out how the elements in the conceptual framework of negotiation are analysed here.

Extent of Negotiation

The extent to which negotiation takes place among teachers on teams, and between them and their pupils, is analysed by looking at the content, the intensity, and the direction of the activity. While these three concepts are in many ways interrelated, for clarity each will be analysed individually and the information will then be combined to give a more complete picture of the dimensions of the interactions involved.

The content refers to the substantive issues being negotiated at any one time. In teacher-teacher interactions these issues include such things as grouping of pupils, procedures to be followed in evaluating pupils, individualized instruction, and the amount of team teaching to be done. The negotiating of the teachers' interactive roles and agendas is intricately interrelated with "haggling" over the substantive issues.

The direction of negotiation in both teacher-teacher and teacher-pupil interactions is analysed by isolating the originator and the potential partisan in each episode of negotiation. The originator has been defined as the person who makes the decision that results in negotiation being initiated, either by himself or by the potential partisans, these being the individuals who are significantly affected by the decisions of the originators. In any situation, the originator and the potential partisan may be the same person. This analysis, however, focused only on situations in which there was at least one potential partisan who was not the originator. The originator and the potential partisan in each episode were identified by the negotiators themselves. The question becomes operationally defined in the asking of the following questions: Who makes the decisions that affect others in the situation to the extent that negotiation is initiated? and, Who is affected by these decisions?

Intensity refers to the extent to which the negotiation is "crucial" or "trivial". In *crucial negotiation,* the potential partisans have the possibility of exerting a fair degree of intentional influence on the originator. The subject being negotiated is important to the potential partisan, and either it is not as important to the originator (consequently, the potential partisan is able to obtain his goal through negotiating) or it is important to both, but the potential partisan is able for other reasons to negotiate with the originator. In both cases a substantial change is likely in the perspective and/or the plan of action of the originator. One example of a situation in which the issue negotiated over did not seem to be as important to the originators as to the potential partisans is described in Negotiation Episode 10 of Chapter 6. This episode points to the intricacies of establishing a division of labour and laying out plans of action for a task a teaching team was to perform. The originators of the negotiations were more or less looking for guidelines rather than attempting to force their ideas on the potential partisans. Negotiation Episode 13 in Appendix E is an example of a negotiation in which the subject is important to both the originator and the potential partisan, but the potential partisan is able to negotiate with the originator and get a substantial change in his original plans. In this situation, a pupil and his teacher were negotiating over the pupil's desire to accompany his classmates on a visit to a local industry. The issue was crucial to both the originator (the teacher) and the potential partisan (the pupil). The pupil was successful in getting the teacher to give him permission to go along with his classmates.

Trivial negotiation occurs in a situation in which the power is firmly in the hands of one party, and the subject being negotiated is important to this party. Even though others in the situation realize this, they still attempt to influence the decision. In such a case there is not likely to be much change in the perspective or plan of action of the power-holder. If those without power persist, they may force changes, but these changes will tend to be formal rather than substantive. A detailed description of an episode of trivial negotiation is given in Negotiation Episode 2 of Chapter 3. This category of negotiation is also exemplified by Negotiation Episodes 15 and 16 of Appendix E.

There may also occur what may be called *extra-trivial negotiation* in which neither side cares much about the result. In other words, regardless of the result, neither side will view itself as having gained or lost much. In fact, only a couple of situations of this kind were noted, and this study does not include any analysis of either of them. One such negotiation took place when a teacher and his pupils were attempting to decide on a time for activities relating to drama. The other took place during a meeting at which teachers were drawing up plans of action for supervising their pupils in certain activities.[6]

Strategies and Stages of Negotiation

The strategies and stages isolated in this analysis of interactions in the school do not involve any detailed analysis of the social techniques used in communication. Only the two general categories of verbal and non-verbal[7] are used, and the activities observed in each are analysed. The study was begun by developing a list of categories of activities in which teachers and pupils engage in attempting to influence each other. These categories include activities that represent, for example, co-operation, displeasure, promises, and flattery. They were developed from a secondary analysis of data collected during two previous studies (Martin, 1970a; 1970b) as well as during the exploratory phase of this research. Bales' (1950:39) interpersonal analysis categories, and the categories of teacher statements, talk, and behaviour developed in different studies of classroom interaction (including those by H. H. Anderson (1939), Withall (1949), Flanders (1951; 1965; 1970), Perkins (1951), and Hughes (1963)) were considered before the categories used at the beginning of this research were developed.

It was deemed necessary to seek a new set of categories instead of using those developed in earlier research, because many of the earlier categories are too general to be useful for locating the strategies and stages used in negotiations amongst teachers and between teachers and their pupils. Some of the earlier categories were ruled out because they are best suited to, and have in fact been developed for, the collecting of data primarily on only one member in an interaction. They include the categories developed by Cogan (1956), H. H. Anderson (1939), and Lippitt and White (1943). Also, most of the earlier schemata of categories were designed to include all types of behaviour in the classroom, whereas the main focus of the research reported on here is the behaviour that was part of, or was directly related to, observed episodes of negotiation. More specifically, we are concerned with the negotiating of interactive roles and agendas in both the routinized and the non-routinized activities in teacher-teacher and teacher-pupil interactions. The five aspects of this negotiating that became central to the study are (a) the ambiguities and disagreements among the actors in the negotiation situation, with particular reference to open and closed negotiations,[8] (b) the power relations in the negotiation situation, (c) the stages and strategies used in the negotiation processes, (d) the importance of the temporal aspects of negotiation, and (e) the outcomes of negotiation processes.

THE STUDY

The research was divided into three phases: (a) the exploratory, (b) the formal interviewing, and (c) the intensive observational phases. The types of school represented, as well as the composition and characteristics of the teams of teachers that co-operated in each of the three phases, are presented in Table 1.

The exploratory phase of the study combined observational techniques with interviewing to develop and test a questionnaire to be used during the formal interviewing. For this phase of the research, two open-plan areas were selected. Traditional schools were not chosen because the writer was already familiar with the general nature of the social interactions that take place in teaching situations in such schools, from three years of teaching experience and two research projects conducted in this type of school (Martin, 1970a; 1970b). The unpublished data from those studies were used in conjunction with the data collected from the two open-plan areas observed during the first phase of this research. Each open-plan area had one team of teachers. One of these teams was in its first year of operation; it had two members of each sex. The other team consisted of two females and one male and was in its second year of operation (Table 1). Teams with different amounts of experience together were selected for the different phases of the research. It was assumed that the length of time team members had worked together might be significant for their negotiations: either communications would have broken down and they would be operating with the least possible amount of interaction, or they would have learned how to negotiate their interactive roles and agendas as team members.

TABLE 1   Teams Participating in the Study

Team number	Type of physical area	Number of members on each team	Sex M	F	Year of operation for the team	Phase of the study involved in
1	open	3	1	2	second	phase one (exploratory)
2	open	4	2	2	first	
3	open	5	2	3	second	phase two (formal interviewing)
4	open	4	4		second	
5	closed	3		3	first	
6	closed	4	2	2	first	
7	closed	3	1	2	first	
8	closed	5	4	1*	first	phase three (participant and non-participant observations)
9	open	3		3	second	
10	mixed	5		5	third	

* The sex composition of this team changed during the observations. One of the male teachers resigned and was replaced by a female.

When the first phase of the research was complete, permission was obtained from one of the school boards in Canada's second largest metropolitan area to continue the research in eleven more public schools. Information on the organizational aspects of these schools was obtained by asking the school principals certain questions (Appendix A). The schools included three open-plan, six closed-plan, and two mixed-plan schools. Three of the eleven refused to take part in the study. Phases two and three of the research were conducted in the remaining eight schools. Only one of these eight schools was an inner-city school, that is, one serving a lower-income segment of the population. A team of teachers from this school was interviewed but not observed. All of the teams observed were in schools serving the same socio-economic class, a mixed class with a middle to upper-middle range.

The substantive issued negotiated over and the categories of activities teachers use in their attempts to influence each other and their pupils were dealt with in the questionnaire developed in phase one and used in phase two of this research.[9] The formal interviews of phase two were designed to provide information that would help the researcher to focus on the experiences of the teachers and the resulting negotiations, observed during the intensive observational phase of the research. The formal interviews involved nineteen teachers from five teams representing five public schools (Table 1).[10]

Phase three involved intensive observation of three teaching teams, one from each of the three varieties of school. One team was in its first year of operation as a team, another team was in its second year, and the third was in its third year. In addition to these variables, the willingness of teachers and pupils to allow the researcher to observe them, and to participate themselves in the interviewing, were considered of great importance. The third phase involved seven months of fieldwork. During his time in the field, the researcher was a participant observer in that, on certain occasions, he had duties to perform in each closed-, open-, and mixed-plan area observed.[11] At these times, as well as at other times when he did not have duties to perform, he observed teachers interacting with pupils. Teacher-teacher interactions during class hours were also observed. The physical layout of the open plan, unlike that of the closed areas, was conducive to such interactions. In addition to observing teacher-teacher interactions at other times, the researcher observed various planning meetings of teachers of the three teams. In order to minimize the effects of his presence at these meetings, he took the role of an observer.

In addition to the regular observations, irregular visits were made to the schools whenever there was a need to follow up some ongoing interaction or to seek out, through informal interviews with teachers and pupils, information about the events observed earlier. All informal interviews regarding the intentions and perceived results of the interactions observed were carried out as early as possible after the event. They included brief informal interviews whenever the opportunity arose—for example, during coffee breaks and other informal meetings in the staffrooms, as well as in the brief breaks between the well-defined teaching episodes of the teaching situations observed. While many of the questions asked in these informal interviews arose out of such things as the incidents observed and the amount of information revealed without further probing, it was deemed necessary to have guideline questions for each episode of assumed negotiation.[12] Since the constant comparative method of data collection and analysis as described by Glaser and Strauss (1967:101-15) was used, other questions were asked when they seemed necessary and appropriate. This method of collecting and analysing data requires a degree of flexibility in the interviewing, to enable the researcher to follow up unanticipated leads concerning the interactions and the intentions behind them. There is also a continuous comparison of data to see how it can be categorized. Such a procedure often demands different questions from one situation to another.

The next four chapters contain detailed analyses of the negotiating of interactive roles and agendas as observed in teacher-pupil and teacher-teacher interactions. The formulation of the concepts developed during the research is presented in this analysis. They are formulated and communicated "by exposition which yields a meaningful picture, abetted by apt illustrations which enable one to grasp the reference in terms of one's own experience" (Blumer, 1969:150).[13]

1. Teacher-pupil interactions have received more attention than teacher-teacher interactions. They are an increasingly well travelled field (e.g., Jackson, 1968; Smith and Geoffrey, 1968; Smith and Kleine, 1969; Fuchs, 1969; Stebbins, 1971), but to understand the processes involved still presents an imposing problem.

2. The team size is known to range from two to six members. The usual size is three or four members. The pupil-teacher ratio is theoretically the same in all situations: team, non-team, open-plan, closed-plan, and mixed-plan.

3. A brief synopsis of the history of the notion of the definition of the situation is given by Stone and Farberman (1970:147-53). The general elements considered by interactants in defining situations have been outlined by Stebbins (1967). The classical statement on the definition of the situation in classroom interactions is given by Waller (1932:292-337).

4. See especially Stebbins (1971:200).

5. This idea is discussed more fully by McCall and Simmons (1966:137-46).

6. The idea that there are at least three categories of negotiation (i.e., crucial, trivial, and extra-trivial) was derived from data collected during two previous studies. Some of these data are reported in Martin (1970a; 1970b). In retrospect, the researcher can report that his reason for not isolating more episodes of extra-trivial negotiation in this study was that he was mainly concerned with interactions more subtle and involved than those encountered in extra-trivial negotiation.

7. Analyses of social techniques with special emphasis on their non-verbal aspects and the close co-ordination of non-verbal and verbal aspects are presented by Argyle (1967; 1969).

8. Briefly, a negotiation is open if no one involved in it gives explicit directives or states the consequences of not following them. On the other hand, if one or more of the negotiators, especially one of the more powerful ones, explicitly gives directives and the consequences of not following them, the negotiation is of the closed variety. These concepts are extensively elaborated on and exemplified in the following chapters.

9. This questionnaire is presented in Appendix B.

10. Analyses of the data collected during this phase of the study are presented in Appendix D.

11. Reviews of selected theoretical and empirical works on observational techniques, and on the collecting and the recording of observational data with particular reference to classroom situations, have been given by Amidon and Simon (1965) and Boyd and DeVault (1966). The strengths and weaknesses of participant observation in classroom research have been stressed by Medley and Mitzel (1958; 1963), Smith and Geoffrey (1968), and Smith and Brock (1970). The application of grounded

theory methodology to classroom phenomena may be found in Smith and Geoffrey (1968:1-20; 251-62) and Jackson (1968:12-13).

12. The guideline questions used are given in Appendix C.
13. The idea of using the meanings given to interactions by the persons observed, to exemplify the concepts mobilized in this study, is similar to the notion of sensitizing concepts, as elaborated on by Blumer (1969:147-52) and Denzin (1970:12-19).

3

Preconditions to
Teacher-Pupil Negotiations

The preconditions for negotiation that are present in teacher-pupil interactions will now be analysed, by isolating the disagreements and ambiguities that the actors perceive in their interactions, and by focusing attention on the power relations that exist in these interactions. The episodes of negotiation observed during this research will be described in this and the next three chapters to illustrate the preconditions and characteristics of this category of social interaction. Because the analyses of teacher-pupil and teacher-teacher negotiations are, to a large extent, centred round the concepts of *closed negotiation* and *open negotiation,* we should elaborate on the meaning of these concepts before proceeding.

Closed negotiation is characterized by explicitly given directives and explicitly stated consequences of not following them. Those who state these directives and consequences may not have the power to bring about the threatened consequences. However, having committed themselves to a definite course of action, they attempt to follow it. In open negotiation, in contrast to the closed variety, there are no explicitly stated directives and no explicitly stated consequences of not following them.

As indicated by one teacher's remarks, there may be differences in the disagreements, in solutions to the disagreements, and in interactions in general, between teacher-pupil and teacher-teacher situations. The first quotation indicates that the teacher sees closed negotiation as the best way to interact with pupils, at least on some occasions. The second indicates that open negotiation exists, at least on some issues, in teacher-teacher interactions.

Sometimes it's just no good to talk to them [the pupils], you got to get tough.

As a team we [teachers] work quite well together. Of course, we have our problems, we don't always agree, but we manage to talk about these things and come to some agreements. Sure we argue. . . . We accept arguments as a healthy way to solve our problems.

In general, teachers are not as a rule as explicit in expressing their expectations of each other (or the consequences if these expectations are not met, or the methods they are prepared to use to influence each other) as they are in their interactions with pupils over similar matters. However, both varieties of negotiation occur in teacher-teacher and in teacher-pupil interactions. The empirical and theoretical boundaries of the two varieties of negotiation will be further illuminated as the various aspects of negotiation are analysed and illustrated in this and subsequent chapters.

AMBIGUITIES AND DISAGREEMENTS

The researcher's observations show that, in order to understand the nature of the ambiguities and disagreements in teacher-pupil negotiation, it is necessary to accept the teachers' definition of the situation with regard to particular pupils. From the teachers' point of view, there are three basic categories of pupils: the *non-negotiables,* the *intermittently negotiables,* and the *continuously negotiables.* Pupils in each of these categories are found in all types of school. Examples of teachers negotiating with intermittently negotiable and continuously negotiable pupils will be given. But first, a series of interactions between a teacher and his pupils will be described in some detail because the interactions indicate how the teacher defined certain pupils in certain ways, and because there is something typical in them of the way some teachers

categorize pupils. They also indicate how teachers allow assumptions regarding each category of pupil to guide their interactions. In addition, the interactions this teacher had with
his pupils during the situations described prompted the
researcher to examine closely the two varieties of negotiation
in teacher-pupil interactions and the lack of negotiation with
particular pupils.

In an attempt to have the pupils evaluate their own performances and progress, the teacher suggested that each
pupil record on a graph how he felt about his work each day
for a week. The teacher pointed out that this was designed to
get the pupils to think about their strengths and especially
their weaknesses—"the areas they need to improve on". He
gave similar information to all of the pupils to guide them in
drawing their graphs. He had individual conferences with
some of the pupils and discussed their graphs with them. One
of the intentions was to compare the pupil's evaluation of
himself with the way the teacher perceived the pupil's performance during the week. Any great discrepancies between
the teacher's evaluation and a pupil's self-evaluation were to
be discussed with the pupil. The teacher noted that his assessment of what the pupils were doing might not correspond to
that of the pupils themselves. During an informal interview,
the teacher noted that there were four pupils whose graphs
were definitely at variance with the way he had perceived
their performances. After talking with these pupils individually, he claimed that he could see where he had misjudged
two of them. He thought that the evaluations the other two
pupils had made of themselves did not correspond to their actual performances. In each case he attempted to point out
where he thought the pupil had not "faced up to reality". The
researcher did not ask to see the completed graphs, but the
teacher brought some of them to his attention and commented on them as follows:[1]

Here are three students [pointing to the graphs of three students]
who never do anything. They did not even draw their graphs. Here's
Leon's, he started it on the first day, but it's not finished. Now here
are four or five [displaying other graphs] of the best students. Their
graphs represent, pretty well, their performances. . . . You have

those two extremes with many variations in between. What can I do with those like Howard? I've tried everything.

Comments from three other teachers are further evidence of the different types of interaction teachers have with different categories of pupil. These comments were given in response to the researcher's inquiries about the reasons for engaging in certain activities or becoming involved in certain types of interaction.

Gladys does not have any good days. Most students do. . . . You can be friendly and reason with many of them. But Gladys, no sir, she's always the same. You can almost tell the days of the week by some of them. [Pause] Probably it's me, but the atmosphere is different at the end of the week than it is on Monday morning.

I have one student here who has always been a problem. [He had been a problem in other years. Until now, this year, he had not been a problem.] I bet you haven't isolated him 'til now. . . . He has not been acting up because I let him alone. He can do what he likes as long as he's not bothering me or anyone else.[2]

I can't relate to Leon at all. You've got to keep on him all the time.

These comments are additional evidence that teachers have open negotiations with some pupils, closed negotiations with others, and a mixture of the two with many. The first comment also indicates that there may be a difference between the types of interaction used at the end of the week and those used at the beginning of the week. For some pupils, because of the teacher's previous and ongoing experiences with them, negotiations with the teacher are at a minimum. Negotiations with these pupils are forced upon the teacher by the pupils. The teacher invariably embarks on closed negotiations only.

Non-negotiable Pupils

There are two basically different groups of pupils in the category of non-negotiables. One includes the passive, quiet pupils who are seldom motivated to take part in any of the ordinary learning experiences of the school. The other includes the pupils with undisciplined styles. In general, the forms of behaviour in the latter group include: negativistic, "I won't" responses to suggestions and directives; a lack of tolerance of tasks they do not enjoy; assertions of independence in a negative way; a tendency to blame teachers or external circumstances when things do not go well; and an inclination to make derogatory remarks about the subject being taught and the situation in general. The passive and undisciplined groups together are only a relatively small part of any class. The passive group seems to be the larger, of the two, with three or four in the average class of thirty pupils, compared with only one or two undisciplined in a similar class.

Teachers reported using both structured and unstructured approaches in their attempts to get the passive pupils to change their behaviour patterns and attitudes. For example, during a meeting with a counsellor, a teacher was heard to remark that he had tried "everything" with one of his pupils and that it was all "no good". He added: "Sometimes I wonder if we are not beating our heads against a wall." The structured approach that teachers report using refers to situations in which the pupils are given specific work to do during a specified time-span. The pupils are supervised during this time, and checked periodically to see whether they are progressing favourably. In contrast, there is the unstructured situation in which pupils may choose what to do from among several alternatives. These pupils are not supervised as closely as those in a structured set-up.

In their interactions with the undisciplined pupils, teachers frequently took the role of an authority figure. One teacher's reason for this was, "You give them an inch and they'll take a foot." Another teacher remarked: "Somehow, I cannot understand Bill. I've tried to be nice to him, but it does not work." The pupils in this group often tried to negotiate with the teachers but, because of the pupils' "unreasonable" demands and "unwillingness to co-operate", the teachers frequently refused to negotiate with them until there was what they considered to be a clear indication that the pupils wanted to change. Apparently, the teachers had developed this stance because of their prior experiences in attempting to have open interactions with the pupils. The pupils, however, were observed forcing teachers to negotiate with them. The subsequent negotiation was frequently of the closed variety, with the teacher explicitly stating the desired behaviour for the situation and the consequences for the pupils if they did not concur. Despite the attempts of teachers to muster all their power and thereby be able to direct the attention and energies of their classes into certain channels, pupils frequently injected their own definitions of the situation into the interactions that took place and were able to gain compromises from the teachers.

Intermittently Negotiable Pupils

Intermittently negotiable pupils are those the teacher feels she can negotiate with only on some occasions and concerning particular issues. There are various reasons why teachers combine other types of interaction, such as bargains and explicitly stated directives, with negotiation. One teacher explained it in this way:

You can't let them [the students] decide everything for themselves. There are some of them who, at different times, will run away with you. Occasionally you got to put the clamps down. . . . Most of the time they are quite good. We discuss things together and I let them have a lot of scope, that is, if they can show me sufficient reason for wanting to do whatever it is they propose.

Another teacher who asked the researcher to spend a few mathematics periods giving individual attention to Lawrence, "an extremely bright student in math", offered this advice:

Lawrence will try to show you that he is better than you but you'll have to step on him. He tries that all the time when we are doing math with him.

During later interactions between Lawrence and the same teacher, it was observed that she was continually attempting to assert her superiority in mathematics. Lawrence did not agree with the teacher's assessment of the situation, at least not with the way she was trying to control the situation. Hence, while they were interacting over mathematical questions their interactive roles were continuously being negotiated. The negotiation of interactive roles during math instruction seemed not to be carried over into other situations.

Negotiation Episode 1 is a synopsis of an interaction

process between a teacher and a pupil. The teacher at first compromised and accepted the pupil's proposal. But, when the pupil failed to abide by his original commitment, the teacher gave him an explicit directive and he followed it. In this situation the teacher was interacting with an intermittently negotiable pupil. At first, she was not sure whether she would negotiate with him.

Negotiation Episode 1

A pupil proposed to his teacher that he would continue to read a book he had started earlier instead of becoming involved in preliminary activities for some projects the class was about to start. The teacher said that he had to sit and listen as she explained the type of project all the pupils could become involved in, and as she made suggestions about what to do and when to do it. The pupil said he had ideas for his own project and did not see why he had to listen to what she was telling the class. The teacher paused for a few moments and then asked the pupil to describe his ideas to her. After the pupil had done this she said he could continue to read his book instead of joining the rest of the class while she was explaining the purpose and the nature of the projects to be done. However, before the teacher had completed the explanation she noticed that the pupil, instead of reading his book, had moved to the sink and was, in her words, "playing around". She then told him to sit with the rest of the class as they continued to discuss the general and specific aspects of the projects to be done. The pupil obeyed the teacher's directive without even hesitating.

The intermittently negotiable pupils tend to experience ambiguity in their interactions with the teacher. From the pupils' perspective, similar behaviour enacted at different times gets different responses from the teacher. For example, a teacher gave four pupils detentions because they were "acting up", and the pupils experienced ambiguity over the teacher's reaction to what she referred to as their "noisy" activities. They pointed to similar situations that had drawn either a positive response or none at all from the teacher. They appeared to be surprised that the teacher reacted this time in this negative way, giving them detentions. The teacher said she was justified in giving detentions, even though the pupils had not received detentions at other times when their activities were "somewhat the same". She implied that the difference was the pupils were not as congenial as usual.

Continuously Negotiable Pupils

There are some pupils with whom teachers can, they think, have open negotiation at all times and over a wide range of issues. These pupils are not given explicit directives, with consequences. Instead, they are given considerable freedom of choice, and in choosing they often participate in open negotiation with their teachers for changes in their activities. One teacher reported that some of his "kids" really worked well on their own. He added:

> They have many good ideas. I give them guidance, but they frequently make suggestions to me and we discuss things on a friendly one-to-one basis. . . . I find that when you listen to them they usually have something to say. . . . They are reasonable.

This comment is in contrast to those recorded above for the non-negotiable category of pupils. Negotiation Episode 2 is given to illustrate this difference further and to demonstrate that open negotiations do take place between teacher and pupil. This is a detailed account of an episode of open negotiation that was observed between a teacher and two pupils with whom the teacher had often engaged in such negotiations.

Negotiation Episode 2

BACKGROUND

A teacher returned to her class after recess and learned that Jack and Joe were "fighting" during her absence. She got descriptions of the situation from both pupils. Then a third pupil volunteered information about what he had seen happening.

PRECONDITIONS PRESENT

1. It was a new situation for those two boys, but it was not

new to the teacher in that she had experienced similar situations with different actors. There was an initial disagreement over the value of the activity the boys were involved in.

2. Despite the teacher's authority position in relation to the pupils, she saw herself as not having sufficient power to realize her aims without taking into account the pupils' perspective.

3. The teacher was reluctant to withdraw without attempting to have the pupils realize that, according to her definition of the situation, they were to behave in certain ways when situations such as this arose.

4. The teacher wanted to teach the pupils to behave "properly" during her absence. For those two boys, at least, she thought her goal could be achieved through negotiations. In an informal interview she said: "It's no use just telling them not to do something, you've got to talk nice to them." Upon further questioning, however, she indicated that for some pupils talking nice does not work. For those pupils she relies on explicitly stated orders with explicitly stated consequences for not following those orders in her attempt to have them behave in certain ways. Hence, any negotiations with this group of pupils were of the closed variety.

EXTENT

Content	Specific aspects of the pupils' agendas were being negotiated over.
Direction	The teacher initiated the negotiations with the pupils. The pupils responded with negotiation tactics of their own.
Intensity	The subject was important to the teacher. It was of less importance to the potential partisans, who consequently made only one attempt to get the authority to change her mind (see stage 2, below). These characteristics make this a trivial negotiation.

STAGES

1. The teacher asked: "Aren't you boys friendly?" After a

brief pause she continued: "Why would you punch a friend?"

Joe remarked that Jack had punched him first.

Jack, however, was quick to point out that it was Joe who started "it".

The teacher explained how much more fun one can have "if you can play without fighting".

2. At this point the boys tried to tell the teacher that they were not serious in their "fighting". One of them said they were only having fun, and the other agreed.

The teacher, however, disagreed and said that fighting could never be for fun, for anyone.

3. The boys did not respond to this, and the teacher did not pursue the matter further.

STRATEGIES

1. The teacher talked "nice" to the boys. Rather than give them explicit directives she asked them questions and, in her words, "tried to reason with them".

2. The pupils tried to explain that they were not serious in the activities the teacher was reprimanding them for. This strategy came about only after they had attempted to blame each other for initiating the activities and the teacher had said that one could have more fun without fighting than one could have by fighting.

OUTCOME

Three months later the teacher reported that there had not been a "replay of the situation involving Joe and Jack". Similar situations had occurred, however, with other pupils.

Negotiation Episode 2 is open negotiation in that the teacher did not explicitly state the consequences of not enacting the prescribed behaviour. Also, instead of explicitly stating the desired behaviour, the teacher asked the pupils questions and explained the value of behaving in a particular way. In commenting on the method she used to negotiate with the pupils, the teacher said: "Some of them take note [meaning pay attention to what is said] while others do not. . . . Of course, there's only two or three who get involved in fights."[3] She indicated that Jack and Joe had not become involved in this type of behaviour before. If they had, she would have handled the situation differently. The implication is that she would probably have stated the consequences of such activities explicitly if she had been dealing with pupils who had been involved previously in similar misbehaviour. Negotiations between a teacher and pupils whom she sees as frequently misbehaving are of the closed variety. The previous activities of the two pupils involved in Negotiation Episode 2 were such that the teacher saw these pupils as continuously negotiable actors.

It seems to be basic to the philosophy of many teachers, although not always practised, that pupils whom they see as misbehaving and/or not performing academically as they should, should be given a way out. In other words, in every such situation the idea is not to "knock him down for it", but to "talk to him" and "give him guidance". One teacher said that he usually tried to create a positive self-concept in the pupil rather than reinforce a negative one, which he thought the pupil was most likely to have if he was always getting into trouble and/or not doing well in his academic work. This philosophy is conducive to open negotiation. However, the fact that teachers label pupils according to the categories discussed in this section is evidence that this philosophy is not implemented at all times or for all pupils.

The existence of different categories leads to an interesting question that this research did not pursue: the extent to which a teacher's expectations of finding certain categories of pupils in his classes are met, if for no other reason than that the expectation is there—a self-fulfilling prophecy. There is another issue related to this question. Teachers have indicated on different occasions that discipline-problem pupils often do not perform well academically. Hence, it would be interesting to investigate the extent to which non-negotiables are failures in their academic activities, and also to investigate whether a pupil was first categorized as a failure or as a non-negotiable.

POWER AND RELUCTANCE

In the outline of the preconditions of negotiation, it was noted that, given the presence of ambiguity and/or disagreement, one or more of the following situations must exist: (a) No one in the interaction has sufficient power to realize his aims. (b) If one or more of the actors has the power to realize his aims, he is reluctant to use this resource. (c) The negotiators are reluctant to leave the situation. These situations will be discussed as they apply to teacher-pupil interactions. First, the power of the teacher and the power of the pupil in these interactions will be analysed, and then the reluctance of teachers and pupils to use their potential power will be discussed. Finally, factors in their reluctance to leave certain situations will be mentioned.

Power

As noted in Chapter 1, "power" is used here to describe the intentional production of a desired effect by one or more actors on one or more other actors. (Of course, a person may have the potential to produce an effect on another without having any intention of using this potential, or he may have the intention without the potential.) Theoretically, teachers have sufficient power to make their pupils behave in ways they deem conducive to academic and social development. This power is derived both from the legal authority structure of the school and from the teachers' expertise. But issuing prohibitions and demonstrating expertise do not always have the effect on pupils' behaviours that the teachers would like. Negotiation Episode 3 shows how a teacher's advice and explicit directives to a pupil did not get the desired response. The teacher in this situation was not successful in mobilizing the potential power she theoretically had from her expertise and legal authority. Intermediaries were employed with some success.

Negotiation Episode 3

BACKGROUND

Clyde was not involved in a certain science project to the extent that his teacher wanted him to be.

PRECONDITIONS PRESENT

1. A disagreement existed between the teacher and a pupil.
2. The teacher could not mobilize sufficient power in the situation to have the pupil behave the way she wanted him to.
3. The teacher's goal was to motivate Clyde to become involved in the project. She had spoken to him a couple of times about this, but did not get the results she desired. The pupil did not know what his goal was in the situation, except that he was not doing his work because he did not want to do it.
4. From the teacher's perspective, negotiation was the most acceptable course for achieving her wishes with regard to the pupil's line of action.

EXTENT

Content	The pupil's involvement in the science project. The pupil's agenda, and to some extent the teacher's agenda, were being negotiated.
Direction	The teacher initiated the negotiation with the pupil.
Intensity	Even though the subject was important to the teacher, the pupil obtained some changes in the teacher's original plans.

STAGES

1. The teacher, on at least three occasions in two days, reminded Clyde of his lack of involvement in the assigned work. These reminders were accompanied by suggestions that he should get more involved in the project and by inquiries concerning his need or desire for help. On each occasion, Clyde gave the teacher excuses for not having done his work.
2. On other occasions, according to the teacher, Clyde pretended to be involved in the project, but in fact he was not. From the teacher's perspective, her interactions with Clyde did not get the positive results she had desired. According to her own assessment, her negotiations to this point had failed.

3. On another day, the teacher explained certain aspects of the project to the class, but Clyde, as usual, was not paying attention. After the teacher had completed the explanation she asked two other pupils to work with Clyde and "help him do this".

STRATEGIES

1. The teacher used two different strategies:
   a) She reminded Clyde of his lack of involvement and offered to help him. In other words, she tried to work with him on a one-to-one basis, thereby negotiating with him privately.
   b) She involved intermediaries—two other students. This put Clyde in a group situation with his fellow students.
2. The teacher's first strategy did not work, in that the pupil still refused to go along with the agenda the teacher wanted him to follow. In the group situation, the pupil's refusal was partly overcome by pressure from his peers.

OUTCOME

The teacher's desires for the pupil were partially met. The pupil compromised to some extent, but only after intermediaries had been appointed.

Individual pupils, as in Negotiation Episode 3, may not have the interaction tactics and/or a career of activities that will influence teachers to consider their perspectives in defining and redefining situations, but when pupils unite they often have sufficient power to exert a substantial influence on the activities of their teachers and on their teachers' interactions with them. Such a situation often occurs when a teacher attempts to reduce the amount of noise being made by the pupils. The following strategies were used by one teacher in an attempt to reduce the noise level in his classroom:

1. He repeated his "suggestions" and "orders" that the pupils were to be quieter while he spoke to them and inquired about their library books.
2. He threatened to keep the pupils in school after 3:30 if they did not listen attentively to what he was saying.

3. He reminded pupils of their previous experiences. Prior to this occasion he had given several detentions for similar activities.
4. Finally, he gave detentions to some pupils.

The outcome of this interaction process may be summarized as follows. Some of the pupils co-operated with the teacher by complying with his request. Others continued with activities the teacher had asked them to stop. Several even continued to go against the wishes of the teacher after he had turned his suggestions into an order. They continued their "misbehaviour" despite a threat that they would be given detentions. Even the enactment of this threat did not reduce the noise level as much as the teacher would have liked. The teacher lacked sufficient power to realize his aims in the situation. He had to compromise on his earlier position concerning an acceptable noise level.

Reluctance

Two kinds of reluctance that occur in teacher-pupil negotiations must be considered here: (a) the reluctance of some at times to use all of their potential power, and (b) the reluctance of the negotiators to leave the situation.

It has been noted that power is the intentional influence that one actor may have over another. In an analysis of the reluctance of one person to influence another to the full extent of his ability, it may be seen that power is a property as well as a process. It is a property in that a person may have it without actually exercising it. For example, a teacher, even when he is not present in the classroom, may have power over his pupils. The pupils are restrained from behaving in certain ways by their anticipation of the teacher's displeasure and/or of the punishment the teacher may administer upon learning that his pupils have misbehaved.

Since only three of the teachers involved in this research had less than three years of teaching experience, we must be cautious in making generalizations about the degree of reluctance likely to be found in newer teachers over the mobilizing of their potential power to influence their pupils. Observation of these three teachers, together with retrospective analyses by other teachers of their first year or two of teaching, indicate that new teachers are apt to attempt to impose on their pupils a social order that they have worked out in advance. References to legal authority and expertise are not uncommon when new teachers are attempting to impose their social order on the teaching situation. In contrast, the more seasoned teachers are more likely to avoid such a strategy. They are often reluctant to attempt to establish their own social order without regard to the social processes that are advanced by the pupils as the teacher-pupil interactions progress. Obversely, there are indications that pupils who have a teacher they recognize as a novice are inclined to be reluctant to let the teacher's legal authority and expertise decide the social order. They realize that they can use the beginning teacher's lack of experience to their advantage in their negotiations with him.

Many teachers are reluctant to exercise their authority and to enforce rules in a harsh or rigid manner. Others are even reluctant to make rules to govern their interactions with their pupils and the pupils' interactions with each other. These reluctances are often based on an assumption that rapport is needed to create an atmosphere conducive to academic and social development and that rapport cannot be established when the social distance between teachers and pupils is conspicuous.

The degree to which a teacher is reluctant to terminate his interaction with his pupils by leaving the situation altogether and the rationale for such a decision—these are empirical questions. But there are several factors that may affect the degree of reluctance in any situation. These include (a) one's contractual and/or voluntary commitments to the group and/or the larger organization in which the situation takes place, (b) one's attachment to the group and/or larger organization, (c) one's prior experiences in similar situations, (d) one's career plans, (e) finding that other alternatives are unacceptable or less acceptable than the idea of negotiation for dealing with the situation, and (f) thinking that the situation offers the only opportunity one will get to achieve one's aims.

Intricately interrelated with the disagreements, ambiguities, power relations, and reluctance to use one's potential power in teacher-pupil negotiations are the characteristics of these negotiations, which will be analysed in the next chapter.

1. What follows is not a quotation. It is a reasonable recall of the teacher's comments. Brackets are used to enclose words describing the teacher's actions while talking.
2. Words in brackets are a paraphrase of information received from the teacher.
3. Brackets contain a paraphrase of later comments by the teacher.

4

Characteristics of
Teacher-Pupil Negotiations

The characteristics of teacher-pupil negotiations will be presented next, by isolating and analysing the strategies, stages, outcomes, and temporal aspects of these negotiations.

STRATEGIES AND STAGES

Three general categories of interaction strategy employed in teacher-pupil interaction were identified during the observational phase of this research: (a) striking a bargain, (b) using other individuals, and (c) employing social-emotional strategies. It was pointed out in the first chapter that strategies are not stages as such, but that they are often intricately interwoven and interrelated in the negotiation process. The stages involved in teacher-pupil negotiations will be identified, as far as possible, in the analysis of these interaction strategies that follows.

Striking a Bargain

Geer (1968) has observed that pupils are continually bargaining with teachers about matters the teachers do not ordinarily consider to be part of teaching. She adds that some of the "rules" pupils make for teachers are in areas that are not well defined, and hence are continually subject to negotiation. It has already been noted that while "bargain" and "negotia-

51

tion" are commonly used interchangeably they are used in this study to refer to two distinct, but often intricately interrelated, processes. Also, as an extension of Geer's statement on bargaining between teachers and their pupils, it should be noted not only that pupils bargain with their teachers, but also that teachers often strike implicit as well as explicit bargains with their pupils. At this point it will be appropriate to look at examples of both teacher- and pupil-initiated bargains that were instrumental in starting negotiations or were parts of negotiations already in progress.[1]

Teacher-initiated bargains. Bargains initiated by teachers are offered sometimes in individual conferences with pupils and sometimes in group settings; the entire class may even be present. These bargains, and the resulting negotiations, if there are any, are referred to here as *private interactions* and *public interactions,* respectively. Negotiation Episode 4 contains an example of a private bargain that a teacher offered to a pupil. The pupil did not accept the bargain. Instead, he negotiated with the teacher and got himself exempted from part of the originally assigned task. In other words, the teacher compromised his original position.

Negotiation Episode 4

Arnold had been working with paper and scissors making designs. When the bell went indicating that it was 3:30 and time for the class to be dismissed, the teacher told him he had to "clean up the mess" he had made on the floor. There were a number of small pieces of paper on the floor, but Arnold said he was not responsible for putting them all there. The teacher thought and expressed the feeling that Arnold was responsible, but Arnold insisted that he "did not put it all there". After all of the pupils except Arnold had left, the teacher compromised and said: "Okay, probably you are not responsible. . . . Probably you did not put it there, but will you pick it all up?" Arnold explicitly refused to pick up all of the paper. Despite the teacher's persistence, Arnold, according to the teacher, "vowed" that he would not change his original plan to clean up only part of the "mess" on the floor. Arnold also said that his mother was expecting him home shortly after 3:30. The teacher then phoned Arnold's mother and related his side of the situation to her. He told her that Arnold would not be home until "five o'clock, or whenever he gets all the paper picked up". The teacher let Arnold leave the classroom at 4:15, even though he had not complied with the teacher's original request. The teacher claimed that Arnold had picked up "most, but not all of the paper" before he was allowed to go. In an informal interview, Arnold claimed that he picked up only about half of the paper. His reason was: "That's all I put there."

Teachers often attempt to strike bargains with their classes as collectivities. These bargains may be unanimously rejected or accepted by the class. More commonly, however, some of the pupils reject while others accept a bargain initiated by the teacher. Those who reject often negotiate effectively with their teacher for changes in the original proposal. The following is an outline of the stages of an episode of negotiation (Negotiation Episode 14, Appendix E) in which a bargain was made in public and the subsequent negotiation was also carried out in public.

1. The teacher told his class that they had to listen to him as he spoke to them concerning library books. He said he wanted all of the pupils to "pay attention" to what he was saying.
2. According to the teacher's definition of the situation, some of the pupils did not respond to his request for their attention. The teacher has noted that his telling the pupils to be quiet was "a request", at first, but when they did not follow the request he turned it into "an order".
3. Some of the pupils continued to talk and move around.
4. Four or five minutes later the teacher said: "Be quiet." He waited a few seconds, and then, as he looked around the room, he said: "A few people are still talking."
5. Shortly after this, the teacher said: "Okay, if you want to talk you'll have to stay after 3:30."
6. The teacher continued to inquire as to who had what books from the library. The pupils were quiet for a few

moments, but, according to the teacher, they became "noisy" again. He stopped his activity and said: "Some of you should remember yesterday." [In an informal interview, the teacher said that several of the pupils had had to stay in after 3:30 the day before for behaviour similar to what they were enacting in the incident described here.]

7. The teacher continued to explain about the books. He was interrupted on different occasions by a couple of the pupils. To each of these pupils he said: "Raise your hand before you speak." After the teacher had finished talking about the library books he put four names on the board for all to see. These four pupils received detentions.

The bargain as indicated in these stages was that if the pupils obeyed the teacher's directives they would be dismissed from their school activities at 3:30, whereas, if they did not, they would be given detentions. This bargain is typical of many that are made in public and are parts of ongoing episodes of negotiation that are carried out in public. Writing the final outcome on the blackboard for all of the negotiators as well as for the other pupils in the class to see is a practice followed by some teachers for bargains and negotiations that involve detentions.

Sometimes, bargains that are offered to pupils in public result in private negotiations. For example, there was a teacher who had requested publicly that all of the work that had been assigned four days before "be done by this morning". The teacher said that when the pupils had finished their assigned work they could move to a different type of activity. The teacher explained this activity to them. They were to work in groups of two or three and they could choose a partner or partners to work with. Each group would think up things to do; for example, "telephone conversation", or "some sort of a guessing game". Whatever they decided to do, they were to write a script, practise performing it, and then present it to the class. The teacher realized that "almost everyone" in the class would want to do this, but the stipulation was that each pupil was to finish the assigned work before proceeding to the new activity. In other words, the bargain was: when you have finished your work you may become involved in this activity. Some of the pupils did not want to accept the bargain. They wanted, instead, to proceed to the activity without completing the assigned work. Three of these pupils negotiated privately with the teacher and got permission to move to the activity without meeting the stated prerequisite. One pupil conducted his negotiation with the teacher with other pupils looking on; in other words, it was a public negotiation.

The common feature of the negotiations that resulted in four pupils getting permission to proceed to another activity without completing the assigned work was that each of the four promised to finish the assigned work at a later time. Two of the pupils, according to the teacher, had their work almost done. The other two "did not have very much done", but the teacher reasoned that since they had been working "fairly hard for the past couple of days" they could move to the activity without having completed all of the assigned work. Thus, the teacher offered a bargain to his entire class of thirty pupils, but it was not accepted by all of them. Four of the pupils then offered the teacher a counter-bargain, saying, in effect: "We will finish our work later, if we get permission to proceed immediately to the activity you just described." Having taken other things into consideration, the teacher accepted the bargain offered to him by these pupils. Three other pupils offered similar bargains to the teacher in an attempt to negotiate their agendas, but they were refused permission to proceed to the activity before completing the required assignment. The refusals were made on the grounds that the pupils had not given "honest" efforts to the assigned work. In addition to this, one of the three had, according to the teacher's assessment, been misbehaving quite frequently. Pupils also initiate bargains quite apart from ones they initiate in reaction to bargains offered by a teacher.

Pupil-initiated bargains. An example of a pupil-initiated bargain that was instrumental in starting an episode of negotiation with a teacher took place while a teacher was testing a pupil's reading ability. The bell had rung, indicating that it was time for a recess. The teacher wanted to leave the open-plan area and stay away from it during the break, but she did not want to tell the pupil this. Instead of telling the pupil that he had to take a recess with the rest of the pupils, she asked him whether he wanted "to stay and finish this, or leave and finish it after recess". To her surprise and dismay, the pupil answered: "I want to finish it now." The pupil also indicated that he would prefer to take a few minutes' break after the testing was done than to take it immediately and be obliged to come back to the test after the recess. In other words, the pupil's offer to the teacher was that he would finish the test if the teacher did not take her recess immediately; at the same time, he would be reluctant to come back after the break to finish it. The teacher did not accept this offer. Nor did she tell the pupil that he had to leave and come back after the recess. A brief episode of negotiation was entered into. The interaction over this disagreement began as an open interaction. The teacher asked the pupil questions and sought to change his opinion without giving him an explicit directive. The interaction never reached the stage of closed negotiation. Even when the teacher indicated to the pupil that it would be better for the pupil to leave the situation and come back to it later, she did not put this in the form of an explicit directive with explicitly stated consequences if it was not obeyed. Instead of adopting this approach, she said in a quiet tone of voice: "I think it is better to wait until 10:45. Come back then and it will only take a few moments to finish." At no time did she indicate to the pupil any consequences of his not taking recess immediately.

Pupils also initiate bargains that result in closed negotiations between themselves and a teacher. Negotiation Episode 5 contains an example of a publicly initiated bargain that was part of a closed negotiation. The negotiation was carried out entirely in public. In this bargain the pupils said, in effect: "If we are going to have to follow a rule, then you must also follow it. If you do not follow it you must be given the same punishment we are given in similar circumstances." The acceptance of this bargain by the teacher seems to have been part of a continuing negotiation process to have pupils remain quiet during the announcements and music that were presented before classes started. In more general terms, the acceptance may be seen as part of a continuing attempt by the teacher to maintain a social order.

Negotiation Episode 5

BACKGROUND

Each morning and afternoon before classes started, the announcements were given and there were a few minutes of music over the public address system. The pupils were not to "move" or "talk" during this time. In other words, wherever they were when the announcements started they had to remain there until the announcements and music were over. If they disobeyed this rule, the penalty was that they would have to remain in one place and "stay quiet" for two or four minutes after the music was over.

A SYNOPSIS OF THE NEGOTIATION

One of the teachers in a team began to talk before the announcements were over. After the announcements and music, the pupils reminded this teacher that she had broken the rule. As a consequence, she would have to stay in one place and remain quiet for two minutes. She claimed that there had been an extremely long pause in the announcements, and that she had thought they were over. So she had begun to speak. The pupils claimed that this was a poor excuse. After a brief discussion the teacher agreed to follow their instructions. During an informal interview, the teacher said that similar situations had arisen twice before during the year and that each time she had accepted the penalty. She reasoned: "We cannot ask them to do things we are not doing ourselves."[2]

Using Other Individuals

Both teachers and pupils use other individuals in their attempts to negotiate with each other. The ways in which teachers use this strategy to influence pupils may be subsumed under four categories: demonstrations, group pressures, comparisons, and playing-off strategies. Each of these categories will be discussed separately.

Demonstrations. On several occasions, teachers were observed to use individual pupils to demonstrate the positive and negative aspects of academic performances and disciplinary activities. An example of this type of strategy will be found in Negotiation Episode 6. Several pupils were not performing academically in the way their teacher felt they should. The teacher's intention was to use pupils whose performances were considered "excellent" and/or "very good" as positive demonstrators to the others in the class.

Negotiation Episode 6

A teacher got his pupils to write poems. He told them that the best poems would be selected and either put on display boards or duplicated and sent round to other classes in the school. In an informal interview, the teacher said that the pupils seemed to work harder and to put more effort into their activities when they knew that their work was to be used in these ways. Some pupils did two poems—one for the display boards and another to be duplicated. Most pupils did one. Only one pupil abandoned his role and did not write a poem. The teacher's comment on this pupil was: "He does not do anything."[3]

This episode was part of a continuing endeavour to negotiate with the pupils to get them involved in a variety of activities and to get each to do his best in those activities. It may be argued that the strategy, as used in this situation, was a demonstration of the negative variety, since it became common knowledge who the worst performers were—those whose poems were not used for display or duplicating purposes. While a desire to avoid negative exposure may have been an important factor influencing the behaviour of some pupils, this was not the teacher's intention. His intention was to show the positive aspects of performing at one's best. The teacher pointed out that, since it was only the better poems that were put on the display boards or duplicated for others to view, it was the pupils who wrote those poems who were spotlighted. The negative aspects of performing "poorly" were only implicitly exposed.

To illuminate further the distinction between positive and negative demonstrations as these concepts are used here, Negotiation Episode 7 is given as an example of a negative demonstration. To reiterate, in the framework of this discussion demonstrations are negative or positive because they have been so defined by the teachers involved. For example, while negotiating with a pupil he believed not to have done his best, the teacher was using his interactions with the pupil as a warning to other pupils to improve. These interactions were also intended as a reminder to pupils who were performing well to continue to do so, in order to avoid coming to the same fate.

Negotiation Episode 7

A teacher told Ralph that his writing was not what it should be. She said: "Your writing and that of others is taxing my eyes. When going over your work on the weekend I could not read it. I threw it away." She added that Ralph would have to do the assignment over again. Then she said that there were three or four others whose writing was almost as bad as Ralph's and that the next time they passed in writing like this their work would be thrown away and would have to be done over again. Ralph attempted to get the teacher to change her opinion concerning the way he had written the assignment, but to no avail. The teacher said she could not accept his "excuses", and she kept to her original decision that he would have to do it again. She also told him to "make sure" that he did better the next time.

Negotiation Episodes 6 and 7 are examples that concern academic performances, but the demonstration type of strategy is also used to negotiate with the pupils over disciplinary matters; for example, the amount of "noise" and "moving around" that will be considered legitimate. Teachers often use a strategy similar to the following in their attempts to negotiate with pupils over their misbehaviour:

A teacher had given three pupils detentions to be served after 3:30. The detentions were given because the pupils, according to the teacher's definition of the situation, had not listened as other pupils were discussing their ideas concerning a certain project. At a later point, the teacher interrupted this discussion a second time and warned the pupils that the list on the board would be growing longer if their behaviour did not change and if they did not become more attentive to what was going on.

The practice of writing on the board the names of pupils who have been given detentions was used at least once by 55 per cent of the teachers who were observed giving detentions. The appearance of names on the board is sometimes intended to be a negative demonstration. One teacher suggested that such a procedure serves three purposes: (a) It is a reminder to teacher and pupils that certain pupils have been given detentions. (b) It causes some embarrassment to the pupils whose names appear. (c) It is a visual reminder to others that, if they misbehave, their names will appear in the list. One of the teachers who did not put names on the board said that both she and the pupils concerned remembered when she had given someone a detention. One reason why they remembered was that she did not use this method of punishment as frequently as some of the other teachers in her school, and when she did use it she displayed great displeasure with the pupils concerned. Referring to one of these situations, this teacher said: "This morning I read the riot act. They knew I was mad."

Group pressures. Group pressure involves having some members of a class pressure others into conforming to certain rules or regulations, or to the teacher's desire concerning these regulations. It is a strategy frequently used. Teachers use it in their attempts to obtain "quietness" before the pupils leave the school at lunch breaks and when classes are over for the day. Pupils have been observed expressing their displeasure at deviating pupils at times when a class had been told that it could not leave until everyone was sitting or standing quietly. The expressions used by the pupils in attempting to influence the deviants included, "Shut up, you idiot," "Don't be a dumb-bell," and "You knucklehead."

One teacher indicated that the rule requiring quiet before school closing was part of the general scheme for maintaining a social order at all times. This may partly explain it, but there seems to be more to it than that. Much less noise was considered legitimate during the last few minutes before classes were dismissed than at other times in the school day. In fact, such quiet was demanded during the regular class time in this school only in the reading periods and at times when announcements from the central office were being presented over the public-address system. One teacher said she hoped that the processes of group pressure would be carried over to other times in the regular class periods without her having to take any steps herself to make this happen. Several teachers pointed out that pupils, intentionally or unintentionally, quite often prevent others from "acting out".

The strategy of group pressure is also used by teachers to get their pupils involved in activities. An example of this was given in Negotiation Episode 3. That episode described the experience of a teacher who, her initial negotiation having failed to get the desired results, was able to create a situation in which group pressure was brought to bear on the pupil. This strategy, as used in Negotiation Episode 3, was partially successful in involving the pupil in a certain academic activity. The success of the process of group pressure, as a way of negotiating with pupils in both academic and disciplinary matters, is one of the reasons why teachers use group activities for many of their classroom projects.

Not only do teachers use group pressures to get pupils to conform to certain standards of social behaviour and to motivate them to work better, but pupils also use these strategies to negotiate with their teachers. On a number of occasions pupils were observed to unite in defence of a peer they felt had been unjustly treated by a teacher. For example, several pupils came to the aid of a peer whom the teacher had reprimanded both verbally and by assigning a detention to him for the part that the teacher said the pupil had played in a "disturbance" in the library. The pupils successfully argued that this pupil was not the instigator or one of the main participants in the disturbance, and therefore should not be given a detention. On another occasion, several pupils refused to participate in a volleyball game because the teacher debarred one of their peers. After a few moments of discussion with the pupils, the teacher admitted that his original judgement might have been too severe. He agreed to let the debarred pupil rejoin the game, but reminded him and the rest of the pupils that some method of punishment would have to be accepted by them if order was to be maintained.

Comparisons. Pupils compare the social and academic activities their own teachers desire of them with those that other teachers desire of their pupils. They also notice the way the same teacher behaves towards different pupils. This may be illustrated by the case of three pupils who did not want to make the type of Christmas decoration their teacher had suggested they might make. Instead, they wanted to make another kind of decoration. At first, the teacher responded negatively. The pupils reacted to this negative response by saying that another teacher's class was making the type of decoration they wanted to make. After pointing this out, they repeated their original request. In response to the renewed request, the teacher suggested that all of the pupils should make the type of decoration she had suggested to them during the period, and she said she would decide later about the other type of decoration. At the team's next planning meeting, the teacher suggested that the pupils be divided into groups according to the kind of decoration they wanted to make. She said that three of her pupils wanted to do what one of the other classes was doing. Another teacher said she also had had difficulty in getting some of her pupils interested in the projects she had started. The teachers decided to divide their pupils into "interest groups", each teacher taking a group and each group having a different activity. Not only did the comparison tactics, as used in the negotiation in this situation, enable the pupils to negotiate their agendas successfully with the teacher, but the teacher's subsequent plan of action had ramifications for all five teachers on the team. It triggered interactions that led the teachers to divide the pupils into interest groups. This strategy of comparing the activities that one teacher allows in her class with another teacher's negative response to the idea of having similar activities in her class is frequently used by pupils attempting to change a teacher's negative response. It is most successful in situations that arise when pupils are involved in art, field trips, or social activities. One teacher noted that comparisons are frequent in the "fringe areas of education". In other words, they did not take place in the core academic subjects such as mathematics, language, and science. Another teacher said that comparison tactics are often used in special activities or projects in which the pupils are given a fairly wide choice.

In team-teaching situations pupils quickly discover which teachers are the strict ones and which will give permission for certain activities. Teaching teams that do not reach some kind of consensus on ways of coping with behaviour problems have difficulty working as a team and at the same time interacting with the pupils. The comparison strategy of pupils prompted some teaching teams to develop a common system of penalties for routinized misbehaviour and a willingness to consider each other's methods of dealing with non-routinized misbehaviour. It has also tended to perpetuate conflicts between teachers whose activities are compared. This point is discussed in detail in the analysis of the characteristics of teacher-teacher negotiations given in Chapter 6.

Pupils, in attempting to negotiate with teachers, also compare their teachers' interactions with other pupils with their interactions with them. They judge these interactions on the basis of their fairness. On two occasions, involving different pupils and teachers, some pupils were observed accusing teachers of being unfair on the basis of inconsistent plans of actions for different pupils whom they saw as deserving the same treatment. The following is a description of the stages and the outcome of an episode of negotiation that illustrates the effectiveness of the strategy of comparison.

Briefly, the situation was that the pupils had been divided into teams and were playing a word game. The team with the highest score over a given period of time was to be considered as the winning one. There was, according to the teacher, "too much noise and moving around" while the game was in progress. He claimed that there was no need for the pupils to talk and move around as much as they did. Having told them about this a couple of times without getting the desired response, the teacher said he would take points off a team's score if any of its members continued to disobey him. At this point in the negotiations, the teacher was applying a group-pressure strategy similar to those described in the previous section. It was when the teacher took points away from one of the teams because George, one of its members, had not complied with his directive to stop any unnecessary talking and moving around that the strategy of comparing was used, resulting in the following stages and outcome.

1. After the teacher notified George that his behaviour had cost his team two points, a couple of the other members of his team simultaneously replied: "Oh no." Colin, a member of George's team, asked the teacher why he did not take points away from the other team. Colin noted that Betsy, one of the other team members, had been "going everywhere".
2. The teacher replied that if they were not quiet they would lose another two points. Colin answered by saying: "She [Betsy] can do it a million times and nothing happens."
3. After some discussion between the teacher and several members of George's team, the teacher reduced the penalty from the original two points to one point.
4. The facial expression and tone of voice George used when he said that this was still "unfair" seemed to sum up the displeasure that was felt by all of the members of his team.
5. After a brief period in which both the teacher and the members of George's team exchanged reasons for their different perspectives, the teacher decided not to penalize anyone. He said he would give everyone another chance.
6. The pupils accepted the teacher's decision.

OUTCOME

The teacher compromised, while the pupils got the changes they desired. In an interview, the teacher said that the pupils probably had a valid point. He added: "I did not realize Betsy was moving around that much, so I gave them the benefit of the doubt. . . . The rest of the game went okay."

In addition to the comparison strategy, this situation also illustrates how group pressure can be successfully exerted on a teacher by a section of his class. Both strategies are used mostly by non-negotiable pupils, often without the desired result.

Playing-off.　Playing-off is defined here as the process of attempting to get one or more actors to pursue a certain line of action, either by intentionally and explicitly giving false information about the actions of other actors involved in the situation, or by intentionally concealing the extent of one's information about the previous courses of action and/or desires of certain other actors, which, if revealed, would undoubtedly stop the actors with whom one is negotiating from acting in the desired ways. The first method of employing this strategy is illustrated by the experience of some pupils who intentionally gave their teachers false information about the interactions they had had with other teachers. This happened in a school where the pupils were not allowed to stay in the open areas during recesses, unless they had permission from one of the teachers. Some of the pupils would stay in the open areas during recess without a teacher's permission. Whenever a teacher asked them to leave they would say that one of the other teachers had given them permission to stay. This went on for three or four weeks, until there were "a number of students hanging around each recess time". One teacher suggested to the others that they should not let so many of the pupils stay in the area during the breaks. The other teachers were surprised to hear this and claimed that they were not giving permission to stay to as many pupils as he was. After a few moments of discussion it became clear that very few of the pupils had been given permission by a teacher to stay in the open areas during recesses. The pupils were playing off one teacher against another by intentionally and explicitly giving false information to some teachers about their interactions with other teachers. If correct information had been given to a teacher with whom a pupil was attempting to negotiate, the pupil's chance of getting the desired result would have been decreased considerably.

The idea of an actor intentionally withholding information concerning previous activities and/or desires of a third party which, if revealed, would undoubtedly prevent a second party from acting in the desired way in the negotiation process was employed by a pupil who, after being ordered out of a gymnasium by physical education teacher A, immediately went to physical education teacher B, seeking and obtaining permission to go to the gymnasium. This pupil did not inform teacher B that teacher A had just ordered her to leave the gymnasium. Having learned of teacher B's decision to give the pupil permission to go to the gymnasium, teacher A was, in her words, "upset, somewhat mad". Teacher B claimed that he would not have given the pupil permission to go to the gymnasium if he had known that teacher A had ordered the pupil to leave the gymnasium. The resulting conflict between teachers A and B was resolved when both of them confronted the pupil and scolded her for what she had done.

Social-Emotional Strategies

Social-emotional strategies have been found to be important in certain circumstances, in teacher-pupil negotiation. Social-emotional strategies include a wide range of activities that are used from time to time, both separately and in conjunction with the other strategies already discussed. The strategies in this category are different from those in the categories discussed above, in that their prime element is their appeal to the emotions. The desire to have alter empathize with ego sometimes motivates ego to express certain emotions, such as happiness, sadness, and seriousness. The following remarks from teachers indicate their perspectives of some of the social-emotional strategies pupils use:

Carl, to cope with his slowness in grasping new concepts, used humour and clowning around to distract me and the class from getting on with it. Some children use humour in a different way . . . making joking remarks about their dumbness, about not understanding something.

Hating to take the time to put down on paper what was in his head (which was plenty), Mike would periodically placate me with an original clever poem.

While various social-emotional expressions are often explicitly used as strategies by the pupil to influence his teacher, similar expressions sometimes unintentionally arouse emotion in the teacher. Indeed, there are indications that a teacher will probably respond more readily to certain emotion-filled expressions if he thinks they are not a part of an intentional strategy. For example, one teacher wrote:[4]

Karen used an air of sadness and helplessness as an unconscious strategy. She had great difficulty coping with life in and out of school. I felt protective towards her and I'm sure she enjoyed it.

Adulating tactics also fall into the category of social-emotional strategies. Both teachers and pupils appeal, often successfully, to each other's emotions. They reciprocate each other's flattering comments on such things as manner of dress and hair-style. Flattery by a teacher may bring tangible goods from the pupils. For example, a pupil was observed giving a teacher some of his art work after the teacher had praised him for his accomplishments in art. Tangible goods such as apples, candies, and cookies are often given to the teacher according to many pupils, by the "teachers' pets". When described as the teacher's pet by his class, a pupil is often the object of much jesting.

Having illustrated the strategies and stages in teacher-pupil negotiation, we turn now to the temporal aspects of these negotiations.

TEMPORAL ASPECTS

In connection with the temporal aspects of negotiation, two factors are significant in the maintaining of a social order: (a) the amount of time it takes to reach a collective agreement on interactive roles and agendas, and (b) the period of time for which the agreement is solemnized (if a definite period is agreed upon). These two are often intricately interrelated, but for clarity they will be discussed separately, with an occasional cross-reference.

Negotiating Time

The length of time it takes to reach a collective agreement resolving a disagreement and/or ambiguity has been analysed by classifying the episodes of negotiation in three categories:

(a) one-meeting negotiations, (b) two-meeting negotiations, and (c) negotiations requiring more than two meetings. A one-meeting negotiation is an episode that has been completed in any one of the four time blocks within the school day, or in one formal or informal meeting outside the regular class hours. Two of the time blocks are in the morning and two are in the afternoon, before and after recess in each session. Some negotiations between teacher and pupil take only two or three minutes. This was the case when a pupil initiated a negotiation with a teacher because he did not want to take the morning recess until he had finished a reading test the teacher was in the process of giving him when the bell rang. Other negotiations take a little longer than this, and some are not completed in a single time block. For example, Arnold's negotiation with the teacher concerning who was to clean up the "mess" on the floor was carried over from the time block following the afternoon recess to the one following the formal closing of the class for the day (Negotiation Episode 4). Negotiations in teacher-pupil situations sometimes involve more than two meetings. Multi-meeting negotiations were observed more frequently in teacher-teacher interactions than in teacher-pupil interactions. This point is discussed more fully in Chapter 6. It is hypothesized that the length of time required to negotiate interactive roles and agendas is one of the differences between negotiations between "equals" and negotiations between "unequals" in all varieties of formal organizations.[5]

The time used to negotiate agendas is intricately related to the time used to negotiate interactive roles. Once a working consensus has been reached on interactive roles, the negotiating of agendas will, it has been observed, proceed without any great difficulty. Where there is some doubt about the interactive roles in the situation, there is likely to be difficulty in negotiating the agendas. Any difficulty in negotiating interactive roles between teachers and pupils may lead to strained relationships. Relationships sometimes become so strained that teachers have been observed to remind pupils explicitly of their (the teachers') legal authority and their expertise. At other times, because of their inability to cope with situations in which they are free to initiate activities without facing the constraints of a more structured set-up, pupils have been observed to seek a more clearly defined structure. This was indicated by their asking the teachers to set work for them, that is, asking the teachers to tell them what to do and when to do it. The pupils seemed to be saying that they did not agree with the interactive roles the teachers expected of them. They wanted more rigidity because they could not cope with the freedom they had been given.

Where a teacher understands and agrees to the desires of the pupils, and vice versa, the interactive roles and agendas may be negotiated in one short meeting. Such was the case when Louis explicitly told his teacher that he did not know what to do. He said: "I cannot think of anything to put in my work plan." Later, the teacher remarked that Louis often needed, even wanted, to be told what to do. Quite unprompted by the researcher, teachers frequently pointed out pupils who were constantly seeking positive feedback on their work. The data included only a couple of examples of negotiations carried out as a direct result of such circumstances. However, it seems logical to assume that the agendas with the pupils who required this type of support would be easier to negotiate if the teacher accepted the role of ego-supporter than if he did not accept the interactive role as defined by the pupil, even though the teacher is formally in a higher position than the pupils in the school hierarchy.

Time Negotiated For

Three of the most striking features of the data on teacher-pupil negotiations, concerning the time for which agreements are to stand, may be stated as follows: (a) The time for which an agreement is to stand is frequently not stated or communicated in any way. (b) The length of time for which a collective agreement between the teacher and the pupils is assumed (at least by the teacher) to stand is frequently interrupted. (c) Teachers often experience difficulty in getting pupils to accept negotiations involving specific time spans. The pupils have been observed to take a "wait and see" attitude rather than commit themselves explicitly.

Despite the legal power of the teachers, the pupils are often able to influence them and have them comply with some of their demands. In other words, the teachers' activities are often constrained by the pupils. The problem of getting agreements and the problem of getting explicit time limits on the agreements, as well as the frequent interruptions in agreements, substantiate this generalization. These interruptions and difficulties are, from the teachers' point of view, often caused by the pupils who, to their dismay, are sometimes "disobedient", or "lacking in motivation", or have not learned to cope with the freedom and opportunities they have been given. These pupils are in the intermittently negotiable category. Pupils in the continuously negotiable category may also, but less frequently, interrupt their agreements with the teacher. Their interruptions are often seen by the teacher to be a result of circumstances different from those that caused the interruptions by the intermittently negotiable pupils. The continuously negotiable pupils interrupt their agreements for "legitimate reasons", and are frequently successful in negotiating with the teachers.

It should be noted that, while the time for which a collective agreement is negotiated has been spoken of in reference to episodes of negotiations that are worked out in one-, two-, or multi-meeting negotiations, many of the episodes of negotiation analysed seem to have been a part of an ongoing attempt to maintain a social order within the teacher-pupil interactions.

OUTCOMES

The outcomes of negotiations were analysed by combining the observations with the subjective views of the actors involved. The observations ascertained the content and direction of the negotiations, while the actors' subjective views of the intensity of the negotiations and the outcome were analysed as such. In other words, instead of using an objective measure to determine how important the subject was to the participants, and who won or lost in the negotiations, the actors' views as expressed during the informal interviewing were analysed. The following question was used to collect data on the outcome of each episode of negotiation analysed:

What was the outcome of the interaction in question? In other words, which of the following things happened?

(a) One person's point of view was accepted in its entirety.
(b) All of the actors compromised.
(c) Nobody really compromised.
(d) Everyone seems to have won.
(e) If the above possibilities are inadequate to describe the results, state in your own words what you think they were.

The outcomes, as obtained from this question, were analysed in relation to the issues being negotiated. The issues on which teachers and pupils negotiate with each other have been grouped into three empirically separate categories: (a) disciplinary, (b) academic, and (c) social. Theoretically, however,

TABLE 2   Issues Negotiated and Teachers' Perceptions of the Outcomes*

	Issues negotiated			
	Disciplinary	*Academic performance*	*Social activities*	*Totals*
	%†	%†	%†	%†
One person's point of view was accepted in its entirety.	50	64	20	50
All of the participants compromised.	36	18	20	27
Nobody really compromised; instead, everyone seems to have won.	14	18	60	23
Totals	100 (N = 14)	100 (N = 11)	100 (N = 5)	100 (N = 30)

* The pupils' perspectives were obtained on only six of the thirty episodes of negotiation included in this table. The main reason for not obtaining the pupils' perspectives on all thirty episodes was that it was impossible to arrange informal interviews with all of the pupils and teachers concerned within a reasonable time limit after the negotiations were observed.

† All percentages were rounded to the nearest whole number.

these categories are often inseparable. For example, the purported purpose of negotiating over disciplinary issues is related to the social and academic development of the pupils. It should also be noted that the outcomes of the negotiations in any of these categories may be influenced by the results of previous interactions in another category. Table 2 is a summary of the episodes of negotiation between teachers and pupils, categorized according to the issues negotiated over and the teachers' perspectives on the outcomes.

The most striking thing about the teacher view of the outcome, as revealed in Table 2, is that, in the negotiations on both disciplinary and academic issues, one person's point of view is seen to have been accepted on 50 per cent or more of the issues negotiated. To be more precise, in at least half of the observed negotiations over disciplinary and academic issues, one of the actors in the negotiation process is seen to have overpowered the other participants, and this actor was the teacher more often than it was one of the pupils (Table 3).

The pupil was overpowered in 73 per cent of the episodes in which one actor's point of view was enforced without alteration. The teacher overpowered the pupil in four negotiations out of seven (57 per cent) in which disciplinary issues

TABLE 3   Teachers' Perceptions of Whose Point of View Was Accepted in Its Entirety

	Issues negotiated			
	Disciplinary	Academic performance	Social activities	Totals
	%*	%	%	%
Teacher overpowering the pupil	57	86	100	73
Pupil overpowering the teacher	43	14		27
Totals	100 (N = 7)	100 (N = 7)	100 (N = 1)	100 (N = 15)

* Percentages are rounded to the nearest whole number.

were negotiated. The pupil was overpowered in six out of seven negotiations (86 per cent) in which academic issues were negotiated (Table 3). When this information is taken with the totals given in Table 2, it is found that in negotiations over matters of a disciplinary nature the teachers perceived themselves as having overpowered the pupils in only four out of fourteen (29 per cent) episodes of negotiations entered into with the pupils; whereas, in the negotiations over academic performance, the teachers saw themselves as having had their proposals accepted without any alterations in six of the eleven (55 per cent) episodes of negotiation observed.

Having isolated and described the preconditions for teacher-pupil negotiations and the characteristics of these negotiations, the next task is to focus on teacher-teacher negotiations, and these will be analysed in the next two chapters.

1. A discussion of bargains that were not a part of any negotiation process is presented in Chapter 8.
2. Another teacher expressed a similar idea when she said that one of the reasons why teachers "have difficulty with students" is that they try to get them to do things adults do not do.
3. From this teacher's perspective, this pupil belongs to the non-negotiable category.
4. This quotation came from a teacher's description of the strategies used in teacher-pupil interactions. At the request of the researcher, this teacher wrote descriptions of a number of strategies, drawing on a diary she had kept.
5. "Equals" refers to occupants of the same formally accepted position in a formal organization. In this context, "unequals" refers to individuals who occupy positions at different levels in the hierarchy of an organization.

5

Preconditions for Teacher-Teacher Negotiations

In order to understand the preconditions for teacher-teacher negotiations, one must look at the problems involved in communicating over disagreements and ambiguities in teacher-teacher interactions, analyse the power relations in these interactions, and isolate teachers' reluctance to use their entire potential power. This chapter deals separately with each of these aspects of the preconditions for teacher-teacher negotiations.

AMBIGUITIES AND DISAGREEMENTS

The data collected concerning one of the teams studied during the first phase of this research indicate that the system of three categories of actors developed from the data on teacher-pupil interactions (non-negotiable, intermittently negotiable, and continuously negotiable) may also be applicable to teacher-teacher interactions in certain teams of teachers. For example, one of the teachers on the team just referred to reported that she was not able "to get along with" one of her team-mates. In retrospect, it is obvious that the two teachers defined each other as non-negotiable. Hence they restricted their interactions with each other to a minimum. Every teacher on each of the teams observed in the third phase saw each of his team-mates as either intermittently or continuously negotiable. The following statements by different teachers illustrate this:

I think we work well as a team.

You are going to get differences arising. . . . That is the way it should be. . . . How can one be passive all the time? The main thing is that we make decisions together.

[A specific teacher] is a little difficult to understand, but I can work with him. . . . I guess that is his way.

Also, in contrast to the teacher-pupil negotiations, most of the negotiations observed in the teacher-teacher interactions on these teams were of the open variety. In other words, only a small percentage of the teacher-teacher negotiations included explicitly stated directives and explicitly stated consequences of not following them. On various occasions, the teachers explicitly stated their expectations of each other with regard to interactive roles and agendas, but the consequences for each other of not performing in line with these expectations were usually only implicitly communicated, if at all. Here are some statements teachers made to each other:

We should go to the Science Centre before Christmas. There are a lot of field trips coming up after Christmas.

If we make the change, I will supervise them [the pupils] as often as I can.

They [the pupils] may go the gymnasium five minutes early, if you let them out of there five minutes earlier.

I don't think you should include . . .

The consequences of not following the plans of action referred to in the above quotations were not explicitly stated. However, the teachers seemed to know the consequences of not following the plans of action pointed to in these and many other similarly stated suggestions and directives. One can only speculate as to the reasons for the teachers' knowledge about these situations. The reasons undoubtedly included their experiences as members of teaching teams and their interactions with the same teachers who were now indicating the plans of actions they thought the team should follow; the situation and the circumstances surrounding the situation in which these plans of action were outlined; the tone of voice used by the teacher; and the nature of the plans of actions to which the teachers were referring. Whatever the reasons, the most important aspects of the processes of negotiation have often been observed to be communicated by the subtle implications of the interactions between and among the negotiators, rather than by explicit statements. However, teachers have sometimes been heard addressing explicit directives to their colleagues and pointing out the consequences of not complying with them. In such situations the in-group structure seems to have broken down. This point will be discussed later in the chapter.

The ambiguities and disagreements round which the negotiations in teacher-teacher interactions revolve have been analysed by focusing on the situations in which they occurred and by determining whether verbal and/or non-verbal means of communication were of major importance to the negotiators. The significance of analysing the ambiguities and disagreements in teacher-teacher negotiations by focusing on verbal and non-verbal means of communication may be seen from the way teachers, intentionally and explicitly, vary their tactics to suit the issue being negotiated. To show how these methods are used by teachers, detailed descriptions will be given of situations illustrating the use of verbal and non-verbal communications. The significance of a move from one method to another in the same episode of negotiation will also be discussed.

Verbal Expressions

Two basic categories of expression have been observed in the verbal communication of ambiguities and disagreements in teacher-teacher interactions. One is the category of expression that explicitly states that an ambiguity and/or disagreement exists concerning the interactive roles and agendas of the actors. The other category includes expressions that only imply the existence of such an ambiguity or disagreement. In order to elaborate on these categories, situations illustrating each of them will be referred to and briefly described.

The disagreements that existed over the interactive roles and agendas when one of the teams observed met to decide on the fate of "the rotary system", which they had adopted earlier in the school year, were explicitly stated and known by all. Even though the goal of each teacher was known by all members of the team before the teachers decided to have a formal meeting to make a decision, each teacher explicitly stated his goal at the beginning of the meeting and negotiated from this base. On other occasions the goals were not explicitly stated during the early stages of the negotiation, but were later introduced subtly to the members of the team. Negotiation Episode 8 contains a description of the subtle way in which one teacher introduced her goals on a certain issue. It illustrates how a great many teachers communicate their desires concerning issues that arise in school.

Negotiation Episode 8

At a planning meeting where the subject of yard duty came up for discussion, teacher A asked the other teachers how they thought it would work if each teacher either went outside or supervised her own students indoors during recesses. She said this would enable the teachers to take their recesses at different times, that is, whenever they felt it would be appropriate to take a break in their class activities. Apart from one teacher's objection that such a system would involve doing yard duty every day, teacher A's suggestion did not receive any comment.

About five weeks after that meeting, teacher A brought up the idea again at a similar meeting, whereupon two teachers offered general comments without saying whether they were for it or against it. A week later, at the next planning meeting, the teachers discussed the possibility of not having an afternoon recess for the next three or four days and, instead, dismissing the students before 3:30. The idea of the proposed change was to enable teachers and students to work on projects resulting from a field trip. It was agreed that, if afternoon recesses were taken at the usual time, the study periods needed for work on projects would not be available. Teacher A again brought up the idea of having each teacher supervise her own students during the recesses. On this occasion, she placed it before the group as an alternative to the existing system. There was considerable discussion during which the pros and cons were presented. The deliberations did not bring any explicitly stated acceptance or rejection of the proposal.

To elaborate on the negotiation between teacher A and her team-mates over changing the time of the recess, it is to be noted that, during the first two meetings in which this teacher initiated the issue of recess as presented here, she did not explicitly state her disagreement with the existing system of having recess at a regular time each morning and afternoon. Instead, she talked about the benefits of having a type of system she was familiar with at another school. It was not until the third meeting that she made her disagreements explicitly known. It was also at the third meeting that she placed her ideas before the meeting in the form of a proposal. Even though her proposal was late in coming (she noted during a conversation with the researcher) she had been "plugging" for changes all year. At different times she had mentioned it casually to other teachers, and she knew that they disagreed with the changes she wanted. Despite these disagreements, she remained convinced of the value of the idea. She attempted to keep the idea alive by mentioning it on different occasions, including the planning meetings referred to in Negotiation Episode 8. The hope that some, if not all, of the teachers would accept her idea remained with her for most of the academic year. She claimed that she did not state her idea as a proposal at first because she feared that it would "be squashed, once and for all". Her strategy was to introduce the idea slowly, and in her words, "not to bulldoze it on the teachers". She also indicated a willingness to take other teachers' pupils from time to time and supervise them at recesses. At first this was interpreted as a gimmick to get the teachers to accept the changes, but she was quick to point out that it was not. In fact, she noted that she did not make an explicit offer to the teachers because she wanted to get the change accepted without having to make such an exchange. Her main argument for the change was that it gave flexibility to the teachers and pupils. She wanted to get the change accepted on the basis of its value to the teachers, but once it was accepted she said that she would help them with the extra work by supervising the pupils during their recesses whenever she could fit it into her schedule. The end product of the interactions was that she only got to first base. Some of them gave a sympathetic hearing to her proposal and agreed with the merits of it, but she did not get them to accept it—not even on a trial basis.

Negotiation Episode 8 not only demonstrates some of the subtleties of implicit expression of one's goals, but also shows how an actor attempted to use verbal communication to influence her team-mates, both implicitly and explicitly. It shows that verbal and non-verbal communication may be combined in various ways to convey disagreement with the interactive roles and agendas of which one is a part and to explain one's goal in seeking changes in the plans of action.

A somewhat different example of how verbal communication has been used in teacher-teacher negotiation is to be seen in the way three teachers negotiated with each other for an agreement concerning what to include in one of the topics to be taught by the team. The goals of all three teachers were explicitly stated and known to all three. Hence, the verbal communication consisted mainly of explicit statements of what each wanted to see included in the topic, and why.[1]

Non-verbal Expressions

Schelling (1960:53-80) has used the term "tacit bargaining" to refer to situations where "communication is incomplete or impossible". In the negotiating of interactive roles and agendas among teachers, as analysed here, verbal communication was possible, but negotiators also commonly elect to use non-verbal techniques to a significant extent, for conveying their experienced ambiguities and disagreements.

There is a certain amount of non-verbal communication in every face-to-face interaction set-up.[2] However, this study did not concern itself with the subtleties of non-verbal interaction per se. The non-verbal activities analysed were overtly employed by specific actors in attempts to influence others while negotiating with them. For example, one teacher, after engaging in several arguments with his colleagues while negotiating with them without getting the results he desired, decided that the best way to deal with them was either to withdraw from the situation whenever the contentious issue arose or to remain in the presence of his colleagues without becoming involved in the disputes. This teacher reported that he frequently avoided situations where issues were being negotiated, especially if he thought that his absence would be conspicuous. He also reported leaving other situations. While avoiding and leaving situations are methods sometimes used to communicate disagreements during informal and casual meetings, they are rarely, if ever, resorted to in connection with formal planning and staff meetings in a school. None was observed in this research or reported by the teachers involved in it. Resorting to this measure would be interpreted as a gross breach of etiquette.

In formal planning and staff meetings, silence on contentious issues is sometimes employed as a method of communicating one's disagreement with the viewpoints and desires of others. For example, one teacher said he had remained quiet during a certain planning meeting, even though one of the teachers had asked him for his opinion on the issue being discussed. He claimed that they knew his position and that his lack of participation would do more to influence them in favour of his perspective than his participation would. He thought that his verbal tactics, in particular his tone of voice and bluntness, limited his ability to influence others during verbal interactions.

Silence is also employed on occasions other than formal planning and staff meetings. For example, a teacher was heard to comment to a team-mate that a third team-mate "does not agree with what we are doing because she has not spoken about it yet". On another occasion, a teacher inquired of a team-mate concerning the actions of another member of the team who was not present at the time, "I wonder why Frank does not want to discuss this arrangement? I know he does not like it, but he will not say so." In both situations the strategy of some teachers was to remain silent, in their attempts to negotiate issues with their team-mates.

Closely associated with the plan of action of remaining silent is the strategy of letting time be a crucial factor in communicating disagreements and ambiguities, as well as an important factor in one's efforts to influence colleagues to fit into particular interactive roles and to follow certain agendas. Negotiation Episode 9 gives an example of this. One of the teachers in this example not only "let time take its course", but also planned to use the intervening time to demonstrate the value of a certain idea of hers for a certain project, thereby, she hoped, influencing a particular teacher. Other teachers also gave indications of using non-verbal methods in their attempts to influence this teacher.

Negotiation Episode 9

At an informal meeting of a five-member team, one of the teachers suggested that the whole team should do a combined project on the topic of "ethnicity". After several discussions of how this could be fitted into their present activities, four of the teachers agreed to have their students pursue aspects of the topic. The aspects selected were ethnic groups, ethnic art, ethnic music, and ethnic dance.

The teacher who originated the idea took the lead in influencing the others to go along with her proposal. At one point she said she was going to carry it out with her class even if the other teachers did not follow through. She said she would "let time take its course". She hoped all of the teachers would become involved in the project after it gained a little momentum.

Even after a considerable time, one of the teachers still did not want to take part in the project. She claimed she could not fit it into her program. After the originator had persuaded three of the teachers to accept her proposal, two of them attempted to get the fifth teacher to go along with them. The negotiations with this teacher extended over a four- or five-week period. They did not produce the desired results in the beginning. One of the teachers said he could not see how the one who opposed the project could fit it into her program.

Therefore, he would not attempt to influence her to take part. The comments from those teachers who tried to influence her included:[3]

We tried to help her get something to fit into her program, but we were unsuccessful.

You can't have someone change her program. It means a lot of work.

She is not sold on the idea. . . . We are trying to accommodate her.

The foregoing analysis of verbal and non-verbal methods of conveying ambiguities and disagreements will be reviewed, the sociological significance of this approach will be further clarified, and the areas needing more systematic research will be identified next, in a discussion addressed to the question of how to achieve a tactful combination of the two methods.

Tactfulness in Combining Verbal and Non-verbal Expressions

The two methods may be used in varying ratio. This analysis will be confined to examples of negotiation in which both methods were of major importance to the negotiators in expressing their disagreements and ambiguities, as well as in their efforts to solve these problems. The variety of combinations of verbal and non-verbal techniques in any negotiation situation depends, of course, on the number of negotiators involved. Theoretically, there are three combinations in which these techniques may be employed as major methods of communication in situations involving three actors. These are: (a) all actors using both verbal and non-verbal techniques, (b) two actors using both techniques and the other using only one, and (c) one actor using both techniques while the other two actors use only one each.

An important sociological question regarding verbal and non-verbal communication concerns the significance of the choice of techniques as the teacher selects a course between the tactful and the blunt for negotiating with colleagues. In some respects, teachers regard themselves as an in-group. They share a common position and set of assumptions until their in-group approach is proven, by individual differences of perspective, to be unrealistic. In in-group situations, the cues involved in the negotiating are known only to the insiders. One teacher's reasoning that she did not want to be away from her pupils for extended periods, and another's argument that one of the teachers had more experience and expertise in physical education than the others, are examples of tactful in-group approaches that have been observed in teacher-teacher negotiations. However, such in-group relationships may not always work, and things that are usually taken for granted may have to be made more explicit. An episode was observed in which two teachers attempted to negotiate with a third, even after the third had tactfully communicated the reasons for her negative response. The third teacher, after listening to continual and persistent arguments by the other two, less tactfully reminded them that the issue had been settled several weeks earlier and that she still gave "no" as her answer. This teacher reverted to more explicit and less tactful means of communicating after her more tactful approach had failed to get the desired results.

In an episode of negotiation among the members of another team, a negotiator who had attempted to use tactful verbal communication changed to a more blunt approach. The agendas of the teachers and pupils were being negotiated because one of the teachers wanted an important change. The pupils of the other team members had been playing in her area and she wanted to have them play either in their "home areas" or in the corridor. At first, this negotiator explicitly and diplomatically communicated her disagreement with the agendas her colleagues had proposed for the pupils in their area of the school. A brief description of the stages of this negotiation will show that the in-group relations seemed not to be adequate for dealing with it. These stages may be summed up as follows:

1. Teacher E had, on several occasions, told the other teachers on her team about the children playing in her room. On different occasions when she returned to her area, there were "things lying around". She said she did not want these things there any more. Therefore, the pupils were not to play there. However, according to teacher E, the other teachers did not do anything about it.

2. At a planning meeting, teacher E again brought the issue to the attention of the other teachers. She said: "I hate to be repetitive. . . . Your kids are still using this room." The teachers appeared to be surprised as this teacher continued: "I do not want to pester you all the time, but they always leave things lying around here. . . ." The other teachers on the team inquired as to the extent of the noise that the pupils were making and suggested that, if the pupils picked up the things they were using and put them in their proper places, they should be able to use this area for floor hockey, etc.

3. After a few moments of discussion one of the teachers said she thought the pupils used the corridors to play in. She added that she had told them not to use teacher E's class area. This teacher seemed to imply that she did not want the pupils to use that area. This was a change from her stance in stage two. She was one of the teachers who had suggested in stage two having the pupils pick up the things they used while in the room.

4. Teacher E continued to present her proposal that the pupils should not be allowed to play in her part of the area. [During an informal interview concerning this part of the meeting, teacher E said: "I guess they thought I was being kind, but now I realize I am being walked on."]

5. The other teachers changed from a defensive position to a more apologetic one. One teacher said: ". . . it's just a misunderstanding." All the teachers agreed that they would tell the pupils not to go into teacher E's class area any more.

6. Three weeks later some of the pupils were still using teacher E's class area to play in. Teacher E did not speak to the other teachers. Instead, she enforced her decision herself. She went to each group of pupils, that is, to each class, and told them that they were not to use her room while she was not there. After this the teachers reminded the pupils that they were not to use teacher E's room.

From this description, it may be seen that teacher E not only wanted the other teachers to say that they were willing to go along with her idea, thus indicating that they had moved from their earlier position, but she expected them to enforce the compromise. It seems that the other teachers were willing to make an agreement so long as teacher E would take both the responsibility for enforcing it and the brunt of the ensuing unpopularity. In attempting to enforce the rule the teachers accepted through compromising, teacher E moved from the tactful approach of speaking to the teachers before giving orders to pupils not in her group to going directly to such pupils and giving them orders in the presence of their own teachers. Such behaviour on the part of a teacher was bound to be considered extremely rude by all the other teachers and would not have occurred in a team with a strong in-group feeling.

Situations in which the negotiators see that the in-group relations are not working (hence calling forth a greater bluntness in explicating things that should be taken for granted) have several possible implications for members of the group, including: (a) retaliatory activities by colleagues, (b) a straining of the relations among the negotiators, (c) a breakdown in negotiations over the issue being discussed, and (d) a decreased probability of negotiations being conducted in future situations. In fact, the in-group structure may collapse altogether. For example, in one of the teams observed during this research the in-group structure was inadequate to sustain a common position in the teachers' interactions with the pupils. From the perspective of one of the teachers, it was unrealistic to attempt to sustain the in-group atmosphere. She said she could not "get along" with one of the other teachers, and claimed that there was "no use" trying to do so. The teacher with whom she could not get along, however, did not see the rationale for abandoning the in-group structure. He implied that all of the members of the team should attempt to develop an in-group atmosphere, especially in their interactions with each other concerning the pupils. This teacher, in commenting on the relations among the teachers on his team, said: "It doesn't make sense. . . . After all, we are supposed to operate as a team. We cannot make decisions on the simplest things."

POWER AND RELUCTANCE

For negotiation to occur in teacher-teacher interactions, not only must there be a disagreement and/or an ambiguity in the situation, but at least one of the following situations must exist:

(a) No one in the interaction has sufficient power to realize his aims.
(b) If one or more of the actors has the power to realize his aims, he is reluctant to use it.
(c) The negotiators are reluctant to leave the situation, and this is because the costs of the situation are seen as less than the rewards to be attained by continued interactions within the group and/or the larger organization in which the situation takes place.

It follows that, where teachers are the occupants of the same formally accepted position in the school hierarchy, no one in the teacher-teacher interactions has sufficient legal power to realize his aims over a fellow teacher.[4] However, even though all of the teachers on a team may have the same legal authority, it should not be assumed that none has any power over another in the interactions that take place among them. Power may exist for a variety of reasons (French and Raven, 1958; 1959). For example, if individual A perceives that individual B can bring rewards to him, then A may have power over B. This is especially the case if A is perceived by B as being the only one, or one of the few, who can give him rewards. On the other hand, A may have power because others perceive him as having the ability to administer punishment to them. Similarly, A may have power over B because B perceives him as having some special knowledge or expertise. It is to this question of power among teachers as occupants of the same formal position in the school organization, with particular reference to the negotiations among them, that the discussion now turns.

Power

If the asymmetrical aspects of power are overstressed, as is sometimes done, one would be inclined to overlook the power relations among individuals of the same status in an organization. Gerth and Mills (1953:193), for example, assert that "politics involves subordinates and superiors". Wrong (1969:46-7) has warned that overemphasis on the asymmetrical aspects of power involves the risk of going too far in severing power relations from their roots in social interaction. He writes: "Asymmetry exists in each individual act-response sequence, but the actors continually alternate the roles of power holder and power subject in the total course of their interaction" (Wrong, 1969:47). The fact that teachers in team situations alternate their "roles of power holder and power subject" is seen in the way leadership is shared. In the negotiations among teachers in team situations, two types of leaders arise, the *sporadic leader* and the *prevalent leader*.

Sporadic leaders are those who are leaders only on relatively rare occasions. Their power and leadership on these occasions are derived from their recognized expertise on the issue being negotiated and/or their successful enactments of persuasive interaction tactics in past situations. The prevalent leaders are more frequently in a leadership position. Even though their leadership spans more situations than that of the sporadic leaders, the reasons for their leadership are basically the same.

The idea of different types of leaders emerging during interactions among formal equals in the organizational hierarchy became apparent from observation of the three teaching teams involved in the third phase of this research. To be specific, if we assume that the negotiator whose proposal is accepted in its entirety in a negotiation is the leader of the group for that situation, then it may be seen that, except for one team, the leadership role is taken by different teachers in the different situations (Table 4). One teacher was leader once and another was leader twice during the five episodes in which one person's proposal was accepted in its entirety by team 8. The teacher whose proposals were accepted, without change, in two episodes of negotiation was unquestionably the prevalent leader on that team. Two of the teachers on team 9 may be described as prevalent leaders in that one had proposals accepted three times and the other had proposals

TABLE 4   Prevalent and Sporadic Leaders as Revealed by a Specific Outcome of the Negotiation Process

Negotiators who have been observed having their proposals accepted without making changes in them	Frequencies of having their proposals accepted without making the changes their colleagues initially required of them	Type of leader
Team 8		
Teacher H	2	Prevalent
Teacher I	1	Sporadic
Principal	2	—
Team 9		
Teacher F	3	Prevalent
Teacher G	2	Prevalent
Team 10		
Teacher D	2	Prevalent

accepted twice without change—which accounts for the five situations on this team in which the outcome was acceptance in its entirety of one negotiator's proposal. On team 10, teacher D's proposals were accepted in the two situations in which an individual's proposals were accepted in their entirety. The other members of teams 8, 9, and 10 were neither prevalent leaders nor sporadic leaders, insofar as this outcome of negotiation was concerned. The sample is small, and we do not have adequate data to permit us to say much about the two types of leaders, except that they often exist on teaching teams whose members occupy the same hierarchical position in the school organization.

Reluctance

In teacher-teacher interactions, as in teacher-pupil interactions, there are two aspects of teachers' reluctance that are important for the negotiations that take place. One is the teachers' reluctance to use the total amount of their power from various sources in interacting with each other, especially in the case of a teacher whose power is sufficient to realize his aims. Another is the teachers' reluctance to leave a situation, even though they experience ambiguities and/or disagreements in it. In contrast to teacher-pupil interactions, none of the teacher-teacher interactions observed in this study involved interactants who possessed the legal power to back up their attempts to exert influence over each other. Such authority, in the schools involved in this research, was reserved for the school administrators, who were not ordinarily involved in the teaching process *per se,* being only *ex officio* members of teaching teams. In the next chapter, we shall see how these administrators often enter into the negotiation process as mediators.

The power teachers have in relation to each other, as pointed out above, is usually derived from their acknowledged expertise and the interaction tactics they have used in the past. While some teachers attempt to create continuous power-dependence relations, only a few attempt to monopolize leadership positions in teaching teams. Also, while it is rare for a teacher to be able to muster sufficient power to realize his aims in several consecutive situations, teachers who do manage to get within reach of accomplishing this are frequently reluctant to use their potential power.

At this point in the development of our theoretical and empirical knowledge concerning reluctances in teacher-teacher interactions, one can only speculate about the reasons for their existence. It may be that there is a realization that power in interactions among occupants of the same position in an organization, especially if the occupants are diverse in expertise, will be of a precarious nature. The probability of any one person having sufficient sustained power to enable him to hold sway in the diversity of situations that arise in team teaching is low. This is illustrated by the rise of prevalent and sporadic leaders, as described above. The reluctance of interactants to mobilize their resources so as to realize their aims completely in any situation may be due to a fear of retaliation. The rationale of teachers not to exert their total influence over colleagues, even when this influence could be very extensive, may be due to a realization that at least one of the team members will very likely be in a position before long to enact retaliatory plans of action. In other words, the probability of retaliatory plans of actions being enacted is higher if the prior activities of any team member are seen as deserving such action than they are if these activities are seen as more or less acceptable. Continuous exertion of one's potential power to the extent of never compromising, or compromising only minimally, is rarely acceptable in team-teaching set-ups.

A teacher's reluctance to leave a situation after experiencing ambiguity and/or disagreement in it is undoubtedly influenced by his feeling that the cost of the situation is less than the rewards he hopes to attain by continued interactions within the group and/or the larger organization in which the situation takes place. The factors that are more or less important to the teacher in defining the situation in this respect are similar to those that were noted in Chapter 3 as being important in teachers' reluctance to terminate interactions with their pupils by leaving the situation altogether. They include: (a) one's contractual and/or voluntary commitments to the group and/or the larger organization in which the situation takes place, (b) one's attachment to all or specific aspects of the group and/or the larger organization, (c) one's prior experiences in similar situations, (d) one's career plans, (e) the possibility that other alternatives are unacceptable or less acceptable than the idea of negotiation to deal with the situation, and (f) the extent to which it seems that only in the present situation can one's aims be achieved.

1. This negotiation is described in Negotiation Episode 16 of Appendix E.
2. Argyle (1967; 1969) has analysed the verbal and non-verbal elements of social interaction. He gives considerable emphasis to the non-verbal elements—for example, bodily contact, posture, physical appearance, facial and gestural movements, eye contact, and the timing, tone, and errors of speech. Other researchers have focused on specific aspects of non-verbal communication. The most noteworthy examples include E. T. Hall (1959; 1969) and Sommer (1969).
3. These comments are not direct quotations, but they represent reasonable recalls of what the teachers said during conversations with the researcher.
4. It was noted in Chapter 2 that teaching teams take one of two forms: "vertical-bureaucratic" or "horizontal-collegial". The former exists when a teacher is appointed by the school administration as a team leader. In such situations, he is given more authority than the other team members. The teachers on each of the teams observed in this research had equal legal authority. Therefore, they may be described as horizontal-collegial teams.

6

Characteristics of Teacher-Teacher Negotiations

The characteristics of teacher-teacher negotiations are analysed next by following an outline similar to that used in
Chapter 4 on the characteristics of teacher-pupil negotiations.
Specifically, the strategies, stages, outcomes, and temporal
aspects of teacher-teacher negotiations are isolated and illustrated in the school setting.

STRATEGIES AND STAGES

The basic strategies teachers used to influence their colleagues in the negotiations observed during this research
have been sorted into four general categories: (a) bargains,
(b) stalemates, (c) demonstrations, and (d) social-emotional
strategies. The stages in the various episodes of negotiation
will be presented, as the data on the strategies of negotiation
are analysed.

Bargains

At various points in the foregoing chapters, bargains have
been defined and empirically illustrated. As with the bargains
in teacher-pupil interactions, those in teacher-teacher interactions have been observed as they were being offered by one
teacher to another individual teacher, as well as by one
teacher to a group of two, three, or four teachers. It has also

been noted that most of the teacher-teacher negotiations observed during this research were of the open variety. The following stages illustrate how this openness prevails in a typical episode of open negotiation. In this episode, the teachers were negotiating their interactive roles subtly as they attempted to reach agreement concerning the agendas of the pupils. Specifically, the issue was to reach an agreement on when the pupils were to get ready to go to their gymnastic classes and when they were to change from their gymnastic clothing into their regular class dress.

1. Teacher I complained about the pupils being late for class after each gymnastic period. He isolated the problem as being caused by keeping the pupils in the gymnasium until the class period ended. Consequently, the pupils did not have time to change from their gymnastic clothes into their regular class clothes. The physical education teacher said that his gymnastic classes were to go for the full time allotted and that he could not help it if the pupils were late for their next classes.

2. Teacher I asked what he was to do. He said he had two choices: either lose ten minutes of his class time while waiting for the pupils to return from the gymnasium, or start his class on time with the result that some pupils would miss instruction. If he did the latter, he would have to repeat himself for the benefit of pupils who were late.

3. Another teacher who had experienced the same problem said she solved it by having the pupils come to the next class immediately after being dismissed from the gymnasium. They wore their ordinary class clothing over their gymnastic outfits, and changed during the next break. In other words, they wore their ordinary dress over their gymnastic outfits for at least one class period. Teacher I disagreed with this solution and said he was not going to adopt it for his pupils.

4. The physical education teacher defended the position given in the first stage of this negotiation by saying that he lost five minutes while the pupils got ready for each period at the gymnasium, and if he let them have five or ten minutes to get ready for their next classes before the end

of the physical education period he would be losing almost half the time allotted for this class. At first, teacher I argued that this was what should happen. He reasoned that since it was the physical education class that the pupils had to prepare for, they should do so during the physical education period.

5. After a few moments, teacher I changed his opinion concerning what should happen and he made the following offer to the physical education teacher: he said that he would let the pupils go to the gymnasium five minutes earlier than the set time, if the physical education teacher would allow them five minutes to get ready for their next class. The physical education teacher hesitated and questioned how this would actually work out.

6. The principal interjected that he thought this was a good idea. After he had made this comment, the physical education teacher agreed to accept teacher I's offer.

The openness of this negotiation is seen in the fact that even when teacher I made an explicit offer to the physical education teacher, the consequences of not accepting it were not explicitly expressed. The strategies of this negotiation may be summed up thus: when teacher I saw that his disagreeing with the physical education teacher's way of operating was not going to get him to change it, he made him an offer. The physical education teacher hesitated over this offer until the principal expressed his support for it. After the principal's support came, the physical education teacher accepted the offer. Even after the principal stated his position, no consequences of not following it were explicitly stated. The teachers concerned indicated later that the principal's comment was taken as "advice" and not as an "order".

Not only are the consequences of not accepting an offer often open, that is, not explicitly stated, but the disagreements and bargains are not always explicitly stated. Teachers may spend considerable time making suggestions and asking questions of each other as they attempt to come to an agreement over the interactive roles and agendas to be performed. Negotiation Episode 10 is an example of this type of interaction. One of the problems in reaching a working agreement in this negotiation process was that even though all of the actors realized how important the task was to them, and each wanted to impress the audience attending the curriculum-night activities, the potential partisans were hesitant about performing the tasks that the originators of the negotiations wanted discussed. While the originators of the various issues negotiated changed their original proposals only after considerable discussion, this discussion seemed to be used more for bringing new information to bear on the different aspects of the program than for influencing the results of the specific issues *per se.*

Negotiation Episode 10

BACKGROUND

This episode of negotiation was enacted during a planning meeting in which the teachers were preparing for "curriculum-night". The program for this occasion was to be completely different from that followed on previous curriculum-nights. Each of the teams of teachers in this school had its own curriculum-night. One such occasion was held each year. The team observed in this study was to use this night to explain their program to the parents and to answer any questions they might have.

In this episode, the teachers were attempting to establish a division of labour so that each teacher would have one aspect of the program to report on. In short, they were trying to reach agreements on how (a) to have "short talks" during the curriculum-night program, (b) not to repeat each other, and (c) to have their program thoroughly covered by their "talks" and their showing of slides. Since these issues were being decided on simultaneously, it was exceedingly difficult to isolate the stages of each. A general, over-all analysis of the stages will suffice here. It should also be noted that the teachers who were making the proposals that served as the basis for subsequent negotiations in this meeting did so in order to get some ideas about the different things that might be done during the curriculum night. They seemed often to be playing the role of devil's advocate when suggestions were put forward.

STAGES

1. Two of the teachers made proposals on different aspects of the division of labour for the curriculum-night program. Counter-proposals of other team members were accepted by the two teachers who had made the original proposals.
2. Even after they had accepted the counter-proposals, the two teachers who had made the original proposals continued to ask questions concerning the completeness of the counter-proposals.
3. Other teachers who changed their original proposals concerning specific aspects of the presentations also did so only after making counter-proposals and haggling with each other. Such a situation arose when teacher D reminded her team-mates in general and teacher C in particular that, since teacher C's proposal to remove certain parts of her talk had been accepted, her idea should also be accepted. Teacher C's proposal was that she should omit any references to specific parents who were volunteers on their team. Teacher D suggested that she should not refer to particular parts of the open-plan area or to individual pupils. Having accepted teacher C's proposal earlier, the teachers agreed to accept teacher D's proposal, but only after considering two issues: the differences and similarities in the two proposals and a reconsideration of the acceptance of teacher C's proposal to omit references to specific parents. Intertwined with the discussions concerning these and other proposals was the question of the length of the different "talks".

STRATEGIES

There was a general discussion of the pros and cons of including certain aspects of the program in the various talks that were to be given at the curriculum-night. Implicit and explicit exchanges were made. For example, at certain times teachers were making suggestions and asking questions, while at other times they were actually making explicit offers to each other. In effect, they were saying, "If you are going to do that, then I'll do this."

The disagreements and ambiguities round each of the issues negotiated in the planning meeting where Negotiation Episode 10 was observed were expressed with varying degrees of explicitness. Concerning one of the issues, for example, a teacher said: "I do not think you should include . . ." At another point, a different teacher asked a team-mate to repeat her reasons for excluding certain things from her presentation. The suggestion that it might be necessary to reconsider an earlier decision was also used to imply a disagreement with this decision. The offers were also expressed with varying degrees of explicitness. One teacher, for example, explicitly said that if another could omit some aspects of her presentation, she could not see why she should not omit what she considered to be similar parts of her presentation. While it was not explicitly stated, two of the teachers seemed to want to take most of the curriculum-night program themselves. On the other hand, there were a couple of teachers who were not eager to be involved because they feared that some members of the audience might ask "unreasonable" questions.[1]

On another occasion where bargains had been more often stated in more explicit ways, the negotiations have tended towards the closed end of the open-closed negotiation continuum. This was the situation when teacher G sought advice from teacher F. The stages and strategies of this negotiation may be summed up as follows:

STAGES

1. Teacher G asked teacher F, one of her team-mates, if she would help her with the testing of some pupils. Teacher F offered to do the testing for teacher G if teacher G would do certain activities with her pupils while she was doing the testing. Teacher G hesitated and then indicated that she did not know how she would work simultaneously with teacher F's pupils and her own.

2. Teacher F replied that teacher G probably wanted to try the testing herself, now that she knew what to look for. Teacher F had pointed out to her the things she should look for. Teacher G replied: "No, I'd rather not. You wouldn't mind doing it for me, would you?"

3. Teacher F reiterated her earlier position that she would do it for teacher G, but only on the condition that teacher G would take a group of her pupils for certain activities while she was carrying out the testing for her.
4. Teacher G agreed to accept teacher F's offer.

STRATEGIES

Teacher G sought advice from teacher F on how to do a particular task. After getting this advice she wanted teacher F to do all of the task for her. Teacher F agreed to do the task if teacher G reciprocated by carrying out a certain task for her. Teacher G hesitated and teacher F repeated her condition for performing the task. Teacher G finally accepted the offer.

It may be seen that in this interaction teacher F explicitly stated an offer to teacher G. Teacher F was willing to help, but she put in a contingent clause. What she was saying was that she would comply with the other teacher's request if the other teacher would follow certain plans of action with her pupils. The consequences of not accepting this offer were made clear to teacher G; specifically, if she did not accept the offer, she would have to carry out the task herself. Having failed to get teacher F to compromise, teacher G apparently saw the original offer as being more enticing than the consequences of not accepting it. She considered it to be a bargain.

Teachers are sometimes reluctant to speak of their interactions with their colleagues in terms of bargains. It is an empirical fact that teachers often offer help, seek and give advice, and become involved in other similar interactions without overtly demanding anything in exchange for their ideas and/or services. Such a situation arose when two teachers offered to take some of a third teacher's pupils after the third teacher had said she was having difficulty working with two groups of pupils during a certain class. The spontaneous offers of these two teachers, together with the information gained during informal interviews with the teachers concerning this and their subsequent interactions, and the researcher's observations on the subsequent interactions, indicate that the two teachers were not motivated by what they were going to get in return for helping the third teacher. The exact benefits to the teacher were not isolated by the researcher. In other words, the nature of the social interaction in many teacher-teacher situations is such that exchange theory does not give us a comprehensive understanding of the processes involved.

On other occasions, the expectation of getting something in return for one's endeavours were vividly demonstrated. In such cases, credit is given on either a short- or a long-term basis and not when the creditor realizes that the possibility of the debt being paid is only a remote one.

Here is an example that might be interpreted to mean that the teacher concerned will not perform certain tasks without the hope of getting something in return. A physical education teacher had asked another teacher to give three of her pupils detentions because of their misbehaviour during a gymnastic class. She refused to do so and told him that the children were his responsibility during his classes. This teacher later pointed out that she could not see why she should give detentions for him. She said: "If he wants to keep them in, let him come in here and stay with them." She added that he was not doing anything to help her with her problems. Similar statements were given by other teachers who had been called upon to help with discipline problems teachers outside of their teams had encountered with some of their pupils. However, when their pupils' misbehaviour was repeatedly brought to their attention, the team teachers were observed attempting to deal with it, but only after making it known to those concerned that they did so rather unwillingly.

The idea of giving to others only in proportion to what one is to get in return was also vividly illustrated on another occasion. Five of the six teachers on two teams decided to plan one unit each in science and then exchange plans with each other. The sixth teacher was not to get the five units the others had planned because he did not contribute a unit himself.

Stalemates

The device of bringing negotiation to a standstill is frequently used effectively in negotiations over interactive roles and agendas in teacher-teacher interactions. The stages and strategies of Negotiation Episode 11 describe a situation in which an actor who was not one of the negotiators took the role of a mediator and suggested that the discussions should cease because of the apparent failure to reach agreement on a certain issue. The mediator suggested that the negotiators come back to the problem later. The issue was solved two days later during a short, informal meeting between the two teachers. This meeting was not observed, but the time lapse obviously played an important part in its rapid success. The solution, according to the teachers, was agreed to "without any difficulty". During the cooling-off period, both teachers had decided to compromise.

Negotiation Episode 11

STAGES

1. A music teacher said she wanted to have a group of "beginners" in music. She wanted eight to ten boys and a similar number of girls. The teachers of the two classes from which these pupils were to be selected began to decide who would be in the group. The first teacher claimed that one of the pupils the second teacher selected for the group was already in a music group. The second teacher then made a counter-claim that the first teacher had done the same thing.
2. The teachers gave their reasons for what they had done, and they reached agreement concerning the two pupils. However, no such agreement was reached concerning four or five other pupils.
3. A third person in the situation interrupted and asked why the two did not notify the music teacher that she could have a group, and defer the decision about who should be in it. They agreed to follow this suggestion.
4. At an informal meeting two days after stage three, the two teachers agreed on the pupils to be included in the group. The agreement involved a compromise. Each teacher accepted the idea that certain pupils should not be in the group, even though the teachers had originally planned for them to be included.

STRATEGIES

There was general discussion between the teachers, in which each tried to put the other on the defensive concerning his rationale for certain decisions. After a stalemate had been reached, a third person, acting as a mediator, suggested that the teachers wait until a later time to continue their negotiations. This suggestion was accepted by the two negotiators.

Suggestions for a postponement of negotiations do not always come from a third party. They have been observed to come from the negotiators themselves. For example, the originator of one of the issues negotiated during these observations said she "let time take its course" during the negotiation process. However, this strategy was not used alone. Having decided that she would like to have the whole team involved in a combined project, this teacher received a negative response from some of her team-mates. She was not deterred by the initial negative response or by the time it took to reach an agreement on the basic points of the issue. In addition to letting time take its course, her main strategies included putting in "plugs" for her proposal whenever the opportunity arose. She also planned to go ahead with her proposal in her own classroom in the hope that this would demonstrate its value to her colleagues. The main strategy of those who did not want to accept the originator's initial proposal was to say that it was too much work and that they did not want to change their programs to accommodate this project. Only one of the negotiators was successful in pursuing this strategy to the extent of not compromising on her original negative response. Even after all of the other teachers had been influenced to accept the proposal and had decided what aspects of the project they would become involved in, this teacher still would not become a part of it.

One of the actors who was in Negotiation Episode 11, but was not involved in the negotiation *per se* volunteered her services as a mediator by making a suggestion to the negotiators. The self-appointed mediator, realizing that a stalemate had been reached, was prompted to suggest that the negotiators should wait until later to continue their negotiations.

In other situations, one or more of the negotiators have deemed it necessary to appoint a mediator. For example, the appointment of a mediator to seek an agreement among the members of a teaching team concerning the setting of a time for a formal meeting of the team was observed in one of the areas involved in this research. At first, the team members attempted to reach an agreement by discussing the issue, but they could not get all of the members to agree to one of the two times that had been proposed. When this stalemate was reached, a mediator was selected from among the negotiators themselves. The basic strategies that were successfully employed by the mediator included giving the negotiators a cooling-off period, and meeting with the negotiators individually. Apparently the mediator did not have to use his persuasive power or any other interaction tactics to obtain an agreement among the actors. The lack of any need for persuasive power to be used while the mediator was seeing the actors individually is consistent with some of Goffman's (1959:106-40) ideas on why "back-stage" negotiation may work when "front-stage" negotiation fails.

The fact that a stalemate exists does not necessarily mean that the appointment of a mediator will follow or that there will be an intentional cooling-off period. It may mean that a cooling-off period will come about without the negotiators knowing that this is what has happened. Cooling-off periods, whether they come about intentionally or unintentionally, frequently involve one or both of the following: (a) Negotiators will assess the available terms of agreements and make additional efforts to bring them more in line with their wishes. (b) There will be a waiting period with no real activity. The choices open are held in suspension in the hope that some new development will change the opponent's mind.

To sum up, it may be seen that, while stalemates may occur unintentionally, they are frequently used intentionally by one or more of the negotiators. In such situations mediators are often effectively employed. Sometimes the mediations occur casually as actors volunteer to perform this function. On other occasions one of the actors is asked to be a mediator in the negotiations. There are several theoretically possible outcomes of negotiations after a stalemate has been reached. At different times in the course of this research, two such outcomes were observed: (a) The stalemate was terminated, in that the actors began to interact with each other again, but friction continued between them to the extent that they did not negotiate with each other. (b) The stalemate was terminated and the negotiators saw some positive aspects to the results. They did not see the results as being entirely positive, but neither the results nor the interactions that led to them deterred the negotiators from continuing to have what they defined as meaningful interactions. The lack of interactions in general and of negotiation in particular, in one of the teams observed during the first phase of this research, seemed to be because the teachers had experienced a stalemate followed by continued friction and no negotiation. This team had not developed an in-group structure. The results of the stalemates in the three teams observed during the third phase of the research fit into the empirical outcome (b), described above. The stalemates among the teachers on these three teams were always terminated, and the actors continued to interact and negotiate with each other. However, in some of the situations experienced by these teams, in-group communications broke down and the negotiators enacted less tactful cues in the negotiation process.

Demonstrations

The use of demonstrations in teacher-pupil negotiations was discussed in Chapter 4. References were made to negotiations in which teachers used pupils to demonstrate the positive and negative aspects of academic performances and disciplinary activities. The idea of demonstrating is somewhat different in teacher-teacher negotiation. Instead of using other individuals as demonstrators in their negotiations with each other, teachers perform acts related to the interactive roles and agendas they are attempting to get their colleagues to follow. In other words, they use their own behaviour to demonstrate their convictions about the courses of action they want others to follow. This strategy is based on the rationale that other teachers may be influenced to pursue these courses of action if one combines actions with the ideas and intentions he expresses verbally. Demonstrations of this nature are often used in conjunction with other strategies. For example, a teacher in Negotiation Episode 9, described in the previous chapter, combined this strategy with the idea of letting "time take its course" and putting in "plugs" for her proposal whenever the opportunity arose. The strategy of demonstrating was not carried out in the situation described in Negotiation Episode 12, but the teacher's expressed willingness to use it was apparently enough to influence her team-mates to accept her proposal.

Negotiation Episode 12

BACKGROUND

This episode of negotiation began at a planning meeting that was held prior to the scheduled teacher-parent interviews. Many of the pupils were in "interest groups" for such activities as needlework, woodwork, and cooking. The groups were often conducted by junior high school pupils and parents. One of the teachers sought advice from her team-mates on what to tell parents who might want to know why their children were in more than one of the interest groups. Some of the pupils were in four or five of these groups.

EXTENT

Content   The interactive roles within the negotiation situation were important as the actors negotiated over the agendas to be followed if a particular situation arose.

Direction   Four teachers were attempting to get one of their team-mates to change her original proposal.

Intensity   The subject was important to four of the five actors in the situation. One of them succeeded in convincing all of the others of the appropriateness of her proposal, and they accepted it.

STAGES

1. One of the teachers sought advice on what to tell parents if

they wanted to know why their children were in more than one interest group. Another teacher did not think that any of the parents would want to know this. The other three teachers on the team thought it was indeed probable that some parents might ask for this information.

2. One of the teachers suggested that they tell them that the pupils needed time away from class activities. This idea was not accepted.

3. Another teacher suggested that they should all give similar reasons. She suggested that the following reasons be given: (a) The program broadens the child's interest. (b) Some of the boys need male attention and some of the helpers from the junior high school are boys. (c) The development of the child requires more individualized attention than the teacher can give when all of the pupils in her class are in the same group.

4. All of the teachers agreed to the suggestion of the need for a united approach to the parents. A couple of them, however, doubted that these reasons would convince parents of the value of volunteer workers, because some of the parents did not like the idea of having other parents and junior high school pupils working with their children.

5. The teacher who gave the reasons outlined in stage 3 was so convinced that they would satisfy even the most doubting parents that she said she would try them first and report back to the teachers on the reactions of the parents.

6. Before this teacher got a chance to demonstrate that her "concise explanation" of the rationale behind their program would satisfy the parents, all of the teachers agreed that her explanation would be adequate to answer any question parents might have concerning this aspect of the program.

STRATEGIES

Some of the teachers gave reasons for not accepting certain proposals as put forth by their colleagues. But the most effective strategy was enacted by one of the teachers when she said that she would use her ideas in a real-life situation to demonstrate that they would prove satisfactory.

The fact that one teacher in Negotiation Episode 12 said she would use the explanation she had given to her colleagues, to demonstrate to them that it was adequate, was of great significance to the subsequent interactions in this negotiation. It served as the turning point in the other teachers' acceptance of her proposal.

Social-Emotional Strategies

The social-emotional strategies are of two interrelated varieties. One emphasizes the negative reactions of the emotional responses that have been outlined by Bales (1950:59); specifically, disagreeing, showing tension, and showing antagonism. The other variety highlights the supportive aspects of interacting. Supportive interactions include the emotionally positive responses of Bales's categories (showing solidarity, showing tension release, and agreeing) and the sharing of workloads and ideas. As noted in the preconditions for negotiations, disagreements are often the beginning points of negotiation. Therefore, all disagreements are not negative. On the contrary, they often given rise to dynamic and meaningful interaction. If disagreements are prolonged and repeated, they may lead to a straining of the relations in a situation. Similarly, continuous expressions of tension and antagonism may lead to the termination of negotiations, and even to the termination of interactions among the actors. Such is the situation in which the negotiators see their in-group relations failing to achieve the desired ends; hence, a greater bluntness occurs in the explicating of things that are taken for granted when the more supportive interactions dominate.

While the supportive social-emotional strategies are often subtly interwoven with other strategies in teacher-teacher negotiations, on occasion they are obviously themselves the key strategies. These strategies are particularly noticeable when a team is experiencing problems over its social environment, including the school system and the community-at-large. One teacher pointed to the problems within the school system:

Our aim is to find out how to operate as a team and give the children a good learning program. The principal comes looking for a cross-grading and the inspector comes looking for neat notebooks and up-to-date lesson plans. [Such] divergent aims were another frustration of the team.[2]

Teachers seek support from their colleagues whenever there is a feeling of conflict between them and the community-at-large. This is demonstrated by the following quotation from a teacher's diary:

I have the feeling that some visitors, some parents, and even some fellow teachers, think the open space concept was the brainchild of the teachers who are assigned to teach here. One parent said to me: "Thank God I don't have any children in this place." . . . It's hard for the team not to feel defensive and discouraged at times.

In responding positively to the need for supportive interactions, teachers quickly negotiate the disagreements and ambiguities that exist among them as a team. In other words, an in-group feeling as illustrated both by the presence of collective agreements and by the processes of achieving these agreements is fostered by intergroup conflicts.

In conclusion, many of the expressions of ambiguity and disagreement, as well as the strategies employed in teacher-teacher negotiation, indicate that compatibility on goals and/or ways of achieving goals is one of the primary bases for cohesion in situations where effective official sanctions are absent. Threats to this compatibility are often taken seriously. The strategies teachers use in negotiating with each other are not used in isolation from one another and are always intricately intertwined with the stages of the negotiation processes.

TEMPORAL ASPECTS

As in the teacher-pupil negotiations analysed in Chapter 4, there are two significant temporal aspects of negotiations which are significant to maintain a social order in teacher-teacher interactions: (a) the amount of time it takes to reach a collective agreement on the interactive roles and agendas, and (b) the length of time for which the agreement is to be effective, if this is specified. For purposes of clarity, these aspects will be discussed separately.

Negotiating Time

The time it takes to reach a collective agreement on each disagreement and ambiguity in teacher-teacher negotiations has
been analysed by classifying episodes of negotiation as:
(a) one-meeting negotiations, or (b) two-meeting negotiations, or (c) more-than-two-meeting negotiations. One-meeting negotiation in teacher-teacher interactions refers to an
episode of negotiation that takes place in one of the four time
blocks within the school day, or in one formal meeting (planning or staff meeting), or in one informal meeting. A two-
meeting negotiation is one that takes place within any two of
the time blocks during regular class hours or in two meetings
outside the regular class hours. In order to illustrate these
concepts and use them to analyse the negotiations in teacher-
teacher interactions, reference will be made to various episodes of negotiation observed in these interactions.

Sixty per cent of the negotiations observed in teacher-
teacher interactions were one-meeting negotiations. Even
though the time involved varied, they, unlike the one-meeting negotiations in teacher-pupil interactions, were usually
longer than two or three minutes. For example, one of the
shortest negotiations in teacher-teacher interactions concerned the pupils' preparation for, and dismissal from, physical education classes. This negotiation took approximately ten
to twelve minutes to reach a collective agreement on the
agendas of the negotiators and the pupils.[3] In contrast to this
relatively short episode, the longest one-meeting negotiation
in teacher-teacher interactions took over an hour to reach
agreement. One such negotiation was entered into because of
the ambiguities and disagreements over the division of labour
for the team's "curriculum-night" program (Negotiation Episode 10).

Only two of the twenty-five episodes of teacher-teacher negotiations were of the two-meeting variety. One of these was
triggered by a disagreement over which pupils were to be
included in a certain group for music (Negotiation Episode
11). The other was a result of an ideological difference concerning who was to do what, when pupils were continually

misbehaving during regular class time and at other times during the school day.

Thirty-two per cent of the episodes of teacher-teacher negotiations required more than two meetings to negotiate. In fact, some of these episodes were continually negotiated over extended periods of time. For example, the negotiations concerning who was to do the physical education program when the regular physical education teacher left took place over a five- or six-week period. On another issue, a team of teachers had two planning meetings and several casual meetings in less than two weeks. This negotiation was to eliminate ambiguities in one aspect of the language program and to solve a disagreement that arose after the teachers had attempted to eliminate the ambiguities.

Isolating the empirical boundaries of the negotiating time of multi-meeting negotiations was a difficult task. Even in one-meeting and two-meeting negotiations, the empirical boundaries (when the issue actually started and exactly when a collective agreement was reached) were often difficult, indeed impossible, to ascertain. This difficulty is at least partly due to the continuous nature of the teacher-teacher and teacher-pupil interactions in general, and negotiations in particular.[4] In fact, the negotiating over some issues is never complete. These issues are either continuously negotiated over or temporarily removed from the interactions to become more salient at a more opportune time.

Time Negotiated For

In contrast to the striking features revealed by the data on teacher-pupil negotiations, concerning the time for which agreements are to stand, as outlined in Chapter 4, the time for which an agreement is to stand in teacher-teacher negotiation is often explicitly communicated. Also, the time for which a collective agreement among teachers is to stand does not seem to be as frequently interrupted as those in the teacher-pupil negotiations. While some issues are renegotiated because one or more of the negotiators fails to implement the decisions that have been reached on certain issues, most of the renegotiations occur either because they are planned for at previous negotiations or because someone expresses a desire for a change in an existing course of action.

The categories of time-span for which collective agreements in teacher-teacher negotiations were to stand and the number of episodes observed in each category are given in Table 5. To repeat an earlier point, the categories in this table are given for analytical and presentational purposes. In the empirical social world these episodes of negotiation are part of an on-going attempt to maintain a social order in teacher-teacher interactions.

TABLE 5   Times for Which Collective Agreements Have Been Negotiated in Teacher-Teacher Interactions

Times negotiated for	Number of episodes
1. The rest of the school year	9
2. One situation	5
3. Indefinite	2
4. Trial basis	3
5. Not solved	2
6. Others	4
Total	25

OUTCOMES

The data on the teachers' perspective of the outcomes of the observed episodes of negotiation were obtained, for the most part, during informal interviews. For each episode of negotiation the negotiators were asked which of the following they thought happened in the outcome of the interactions:

(a) One person's point of view got accepted in its entirety.

(b) All of the actors compromised.

(c) Nobody really compromised.

(d) Everyone seems to have won.

(e) If the above possibilities are inadequate to describe the results, state in your words what you think they were.

Before discussing the data concerning the outcomes of the negotiations in teacher-teacher interactions, as obtained by this question, it will be appropriate to define "consensus" as it has been used in analysing the outcomes of these negotiations. Scheff (1967) has pointed out the distinction between the "individual-agreement" definition of consensus and the "co-orientation" definition. In this analysis, the individual-agreement definition of consensus has been employed. Individual agreement refers to the degree of agreement among the negotiators involved in each episode of negotiation concerning the outcome of the negotiation processes.

One of the significant features of the data on outcomes is that in thirteen of the twenty-five episodes of negotiation observed, some, if not all, of the negotiators perceived the outcomes in terms of everyone in the situation winning. Even some of those who said that one person's point of view was accepted in its entirety also saw everyone winning. In five of the negotiations, at least one of the negotiators saw himself and his fellow negotiators as simultaneously compromising and winning in their interactions. This seemingly contradictory view of the outcomes was explained by the negotiators when they pointed out that they saw themselves and others as compromising insofar as their original proposals were concerned, but gaining in the final results. The gains were seen by retrospective analysis of the interactions concerned. This finding shows the importance of a subjective view of the results of negotiations. If one is to get a comprehensive understanding of the interactions in general, and of the negotiations in particular, in any situation, it is not sufficient to rely entirely on some objective construct for measuring the outcomes. The negotiators' view of the outcomes must also be made an important part of one's analysis, because this perspective is salient in their subsequent interactions and negotiations.

Another interesting finding from the analysis of the outcomes of teacher-teacher negotiations is the high degree of individual agreement in the perceived outcomes of the negotiations. In sixteen of the twenty-five episodes observed, the negotiators were in total agreement concerning the results. Some of them were in total agreement that everyone won in certain episodes of negotiation. It is obvious that, for many of the negotiators, winning and losing did not imply a zero sum game. It was not winning relative to an adversary or friend whom one may not want to deprive while gaining something for one's self. Instead, it meant winning relative to one's own value system or to a third party not present at the time. The existence of prevalent and sporadic leaders, as discussed in Chapter 5, indicates that no single negotiator controls many consecutive situations in the negotiations among teachers. Teacher-teacher situations give rise to dynamic interactions that can be understood only by using a language of political process that emphasizes negotiations.

We now turn to some of the issues worthy of note by way of comparing the interactions in different types of school. A summary of the findings in teacher-pupil and teacher-teacher negotiations, as they are related to the social structure of teaching situations, will also be presented in the next chapter.

1. This fear was created by the fact that, at an earlier curriculum-night of another team in this school, a parent in the audience was seen as a "trouble maker" in that she asked questions that were not, from the teachers' perspective, relevent to the situation.
2. This quotation was taken from a teacher's description of the problems she experienced while working on a teaching team.
3. The stages of this negotiation are outlined at the beginning of this chapter.
4. This problem also arose when an attempt was made to isolate episodes of interaction other than negotiations. Analyses of these episodes of interaction will be presented in Chapter 8.

7

The Social Structure of Teaching Situations

"Social structure" is used to refer "to an arrangement of configuration of social activities that is seen to exist over some period of time and that is believed to depict underlying patterns of social order" (Olsen, 1968:46). In teaching situations, both teachers and pupils must play their parts within certain boundaries. These boundaries are not always clearly defined in that they are flexible and sometimes negotiable. They generally include the more or less bureaucratic framework of the school and the boundaries of physical space. While interacting within the confines of these sometimes general boundaries, the actors arrive at general and specific arrangements for their individual and collective activities. These arrangements determine the social structure of the teaching situations. This social structure will be presented here by comparing the negotiations in the different types of schools represented in this research, and by summarizing the findings of this research that speak to the social structure of these setups.

SCHOOL TYPES: A COMPARISON
Following the sequence of analyses of the foregoing chapters, this section will first compare the teacher-pupil interactions in the different schools and then move to the teacher-teacher interactions in these schools.

Teacher-Pupil Interactions

The impression frequently created by the literature on open-plan areas is that the teacher-pupil interactions are somehow radically different from the interactions to be found in the classroom-type structure.[1] The greatest difference between these schools may, however, be in their architectural designs. The type of architecture does not necessarily indicate the nature of the interactions that take place. While certain types of physical structure may be more conducive to certain aspects of interaction than others, one should not be led to assume that architecture means everything. "Open education", that is, individualized programs and flexible scheduling, may also be implemented in classroom situations. This study has not been able to isolate any significant differences in the negotiations that go on between teachers and pupils in the three types of school structures observed—open, closed, and mixed. The similarities between these types of schools will be illustrated by giving a brief summary of the key findings concerning the ambiguities, disagreements, stages, strategies, temporal aspects, and outcomes of the negotiations observed between the teachers and the pupils.

It has been demonstrated that both open and closed negotiations are found in all three types of school. Also, each teacher has pupils whom he describes as non-negotiables, intermittently negotiables, and continuously negotiables. Concerning the specific interaction tactics, the formal interviewing of teachers showed that there was very little difference in the reported frequency with which teachers act in the different structures (Table 11, Appendix D). The three activities that showed the greatest differences, in the data from these interviews, were: making a joke out of the situation when many of the participants in the situation thought it to be a serious one, making promises, and showing displeasures. The data on the negotiations from the intensive observational phase of the research did not seem to indicate that these tactics were used any more frequently in one type of school than in another. We must be cautious, and emphasize "do not seem to indicate", because this research was not concerned with the frequency of negotiations *per se,* but with developing empirical and theoretical categories of certain aspects of the processes involved in the negotiations that take place in teacher-pupil interactions. Teachers and pupils in schools of all three designs initiated bargains with each other that, at various times, either initiated or were parts of on-going episodes of negotiation. Teachers were also observed using pupils for demonstrations and using groups of pupils to apply pressure on individual pupils or groups of pupils whom they were having difficulty influencing. Pupils in each of the schools were observed attempting to use the actions of other teachers to strengthen their negotiating positions with teachers with whom they were negotiating. All of the schools had pupils who attempted to play one teacher off against another to get a desired response from a teacher.

The negotiations between the teachers and pupils in all of the schools centred round the three general issues of disciplinary, academic, and social activities, but the differing spatial relationships meant that some of the specific issues varied from school to school. Even with these differences, the processes involved in the negotiations are similar for all three types of school.

Teacher-Teacher Interactions

It has been noted that pupils in the open-plan school may have interactions with a larger number of pupils during regular class time than their counterparts in the closed school. Similarly, the lack of walls in the open-plan school permits teachers to interact more frequently during regular class hours than they can in the classroom set-up. In fact, the teachers in closed schools see each other only on rare occasions during the regular class hours. Even when they do interact during those hours, their interactions are usually nothing more than a greeting. Hence, for the most part, the teachers in closed schools can only negotiate with each other outside regular class hours. However, it should not be assumed that the absence of physical walls in open-plan schools automatically means more interaction or that the interaction is somehow different from what occurs in the classroom type of school. Some writers have made this assumption. For example, Cohen (1973:147) took "the distinction between the open-space school and the conventional school" as "a rough indicator of differences in the probability of receiving praise and support from colleagues and differences in the probability of playing an influential role among colleagues". On the other hand, Bunyan (1967) has pointed out that the desire to teach co-operatively is more important to an open climate for interaction than the kind of building or the equipment available. The presence or absence of walls may or may not have a bearing on the frequency of interaction among teachers or on the issues over which the interactions take place. The teachers in one of the open areas studied during the first phase of this research had obviously built invisible walls. They had no verbal interactions with each other during regular class time. The invisible walls were also known to the pupils, because they, too, were confined to certain parts of the areas where their teachers performed. Even outside regular class hours, this team of teachers had a minimum of interaction. In contrast, the team of teachers in the classroom type of school observed in the third phase of this research had a considerable amount of interaction in their frequent unscheduled planning meetings and in their occasional scheduled planning meetings.

It is obvious that while the architecture of a school may be important to the frequency of the teacher-teacher interaction, other variables are often of greater importance. Variables other than architecture often account for the construction of invisible walls and the respect given to these walls. Included in these variables is the organizational structure of teachers as staff members (that is, the degree to which they are performing as a team, and not as individuals) and the nature and amount of in-service training given to the teachers who move from non-team structures to team structures. The extent to which beginning teachers have had training oriented towards team teaching is also an important variable. Many teacher-training programs are still oriented towards training teachers to perform as individuals and not as members of teams. Another crucial variable is the process of selecting teachers to work as team members. It is suggested here that these variables have important consequences for the interactions that take place in all types of school. In other words, the construction of a physically open area is not sufficient to counteract the factors that frequently militate against team teaching and other situations conducive to receiving praise, respect, and support from one's colleagues concerning school activities.

While this study did not concern itself with recording the frequencies of interaction in each type of school area observed during or outside regular class hours, it appears that the frequency of teacher-teacher interaction outside regular class hours was about the same for all areas. The open-plan areas generally had the most teacher-teacher interaction during regular class hours. Despite this apparent difference in frequency and regularity of interaction, when the processes of negotiation are isolated for each type of school it may be seen that there are many similarities. Even though our sample of negotiations in teacher-teacher interactions is too small to say that there are absolutely no differences in the teacher-teacher negotiations between the different types of school, several significant similarities have been observed in the informal negotiations that take place in teacher-teacher interactions in the different types. These similarities have been presented in various parts of this book under the headings "ambiguities and disagreements", "power and reluctance", "strategies and stages", "temporal aspects", and "outcomes".

The significance of the findings on negotiations for our understanding of the social structure of teaching situations will now be presented.[2]

SUMMARY

The insights gained into the social structure of teaching situations from the teacher-pupil and teacher-teacher negotiations analysed in this research may be summed up as follows:

1. The interactions between the occupants of the teacher and pupil statuses and among the occupants of the teacher status are not entirely determined by the positions themselves. For example, teachers' interactions with their pupils are based not only on the fact that they are pupils, but also on

whether they are non-negotiable, intermittently negotiable, or continuously negotiable pupils. The social distance that is maintained between teachers and pupils is different for each category of pupils.

2. Social control in the school is maintained through the implementation of both open and closed negotiations.

3. Whatever the category of pupils, when a teacher views an episode of negotiation as being unsuccessful in achieving his desired end he will, more often than not, terminate the negotiation. Termination occurs most often in teachers' interactions with the non-negotiables, and least often in their interactions with the continuously negotiables. This in itself may be an indication that teachers see their negotiations with the continuously negotiables as being successful more often than their negotiations with the intermittently negotiables.

4. In situations in which the greatest potential power is clearly in the hands of one person, this person is often reluctant to use it. This reluctance exists regardless of the source of power.

5. In the absence of effective sanctions through authority (for example, in teacher-teacher interactions) compatibility on acceptance of courses of action is the primary basis for cohesion. Threats to this compatibility are often taken seriously. Consequently, such threats play an important role in the dynamics of the interactions in those situations.

6. While interacting with each other, teachers are often able to influence each other's decisions concerning the activities of members of the teaching team. Some teachers, in these interactions, emerge as either prevalent leaders or sporadic leaders. It is these leaders who have the greatest influence on the decisions made.

7. Some pupils are also able to influence teachers' decisions. Therefore, in teacher-pupil interactions there is often a working out by teachers and pupils of courses of action in terms of the needs and desires of all parties in the interactions. In both teacher-teacher and teacher-pupil interactions some of the negotiations are of the trivial variety. In other words, one actor has sufficient potential power to achieve his aims in the situation and he uses it, often with reluctance, to

achieve this end. Consequently, other actors in the situation have little influence on the decisions made.

8. Bargains, group pressures, demonstrations, comparisons, playing-off, and social-emotional strategies are often used in teacher-pupil negotiations; bargains, stalemates, demonstrations, and social-emotional strategies are the most important strategies in teacher-teacher negotiations.

9. Generally speaking, there are differences in negotiating time between teacher-teacher negotiations and teacher-pupil negotiations. More meetings, and more time within these meetings, are usually required to reach the final outcome in teacher-teacher negotiations than are required to reach an outcome in teacher-pupil negotiations.

10. The period for which an agreement in teacher-pupil negotiations is assumed, at least by the teacher, to stand is frequently interrupted. In contrast, the period for which a collective agreement among teachers is to stand is usually not interrupted.

11. The frequent interruptions in the periods for which agreements are to stand in teacher-pupil negotiations and the emergence of sporadic and prevalent leaders in teacher-teacher negotiations are two indications of the dynamics of the social structures in teaching situations.

Up to this point, we have focused our attention entirely on negotiations. One might be inclined to ask what there is in teacher-pupil and teacher-teacher interactions that is not negotiation. How can one isolate the other categories of interaction? In answer to these questions, the distinctiveness of negotiation in interactions in the school setting will be discussed in the next chapter.

1. See, for example, Goss (1965), Barton (1968), Ingalls (1969), McNutt (1969), and Wilson, Langevin, and Stuckey (1969).
2. Theorizations concerning the applicability of a negotiation perspective to understanding the social structure of formal organization settings other than those found in the school are given in Chapter 9, in the section on "Negotiating Interactive Roles and Agendas".

8

The Distinctiveness of Negotiation

In order to show the distinctiveness of negotiation, among other closely related episodes of interaction in teacher-pupil and teacher-teacher situations, this chapter will concentrate on interactions that meet some, but not all, of the preconditions of negotiation. The intent is to show that some interactions are in many aspects similar to negotiations, yet they are not classified as such because all of the preconditions of this variety of interaction are not met. From a sorting out of the multitude of episodes of interaction among teachers and between teachers and pupils, a typology of seven interrelated categories was developed.[1]

  I. Observed in both teacher-pupil and teacher-teacher interactions
    1. Negotiations
    2. Bargains
    3. Seeking and/or giving advice
    4. General discussions
    5. Questions and answers
 II. Observed only in teacher-pupil interactions
    6. Teacher giving explicit directives to pupils
    7. Pupils abandoning their roles

These categories of social interaction were frequently

related to negotiation in that they were observed on different occasions to be parts of the negotiation process. At other times, they were enacted without being a part of any observed negotiation. To further delineate the empirical boundaries of negotiation, activities in each of these categories will be illustrated and analysed with respect to the presence or absence of the preconditions of negotiation as given in our conceptual framework.

TEACHER-PUPIL AND TEACHER-TEACHER INTERACTIONS

The four categories of interaction to be analysed here are (a) bargains, (b) seeking and/or giving advice, (c) general discussions, and (d) questions and answers. The examples given in each category are peripheral to negotiation in that some but not all of the preconditions of this category of interaction are present.

Bargains

The intricateness of the relationship between a bargain and an episode of negotiation was discussed at some length in earlier chapters. It was seen that on different occasions bargains may or may not be instrumental in initiating negotiation or be part of an on-going episode of negotiation. In the analysis of bargains that were parts of negotiations, it was seen that there are major differences between those that are parts of open negotiations and those that are parts of closed negotiations. The bargains that were not a part of any observed negotiations, however, were frequently similar to those that had been observed to be parts of various episodes of negotiations. In fact, similar bargains offered in different situations and to different actors had different effects on subsequent interactions. On some occasions they seemed to be intricately interwoven with the processes of negotiating while on other occasions they were not, or at least not obviously, interrelated to those processes. For example, bargains 1 and 2 in Table 6 were observed at different times as being outside of any negotiation process and as being a part of an episode of negotiation. As in previous chapters, teacher-pupil and teacher-teacher bargains will be presented separately here.

TABLE 6   Analysis of Non-Negotiated Bargains Initiated by Teachers in Teacher-Pupil Interactions

	Choice of activities offered to the pupils	Rewards	Punishments
Bargain No. 1*	To be quiet To continue to be noisy	Not to be given a detention	To be given a detention
Bargain No. 2*	To present written work in a neater form To continue to be "sloppy" in doing written work	To receive the approval of the teacher	To have this messy work shown to the class
Bargain No. 3	To apologize to the vice-principal Not to apologize to the vice-principal	To be given permission to go back to the classroom	To sit on the bench by the central office of the school until he apologizes
Bargain No. 4	To stop flicking paper-clips To continue to flick paper-clips	To be permitted to stay in the classroom with the other pupils	To be sent home for the rest of the morning session
Bargain No. 5	To spend, in the teacher's words, "a reasonable amount of time at the library" Either to go to the library too frequently, or to spend too long there	To continue to have library privileges	To be deprived of library privileges

*Bargains similar to these have been observed to be the immediate causes of negotiations.

Teacher-pupil bargains.   To reiterate the distinction between a bargain and an episode of negotiation, it is important to note that a bargain is an exchange of social objects at a cost that is considered to be favourable by at least one of the parties involved, whereas a negotiation is a much broader process that includes haggling over the acceptance or rejection of the bargain. Negotiation takes place only after one of the actors does not wish to accept the offer as it is and thereby attempts to change it. In addition, the other actor must be willing or forced to reconsider his offer. Teachers have been observed to offer to their pupils what they consider to be bargains and then to refuse to negotiate over them, even though the pupils have attempted to do so. The following is an example of such a situation:

The teacher brought a spirograph to the class. While he was demonstrating how it works, two of the pupils asked if they could use it. The teacher replied by directing his response to the entire class. He said: "I'll let each of you make a spirograph next week if you get a perfect spelling." When the next spelling test came, several of the pupils did not get a "perfect spelling", but they wanted to make a spirograph. The teacher said "no" to their requests because they had not met the requirement he had set for them. He refused to negotiate the bargain he had offered the pupils.

On other occasions teachers have offered what they considered to be bargains to pupils who have accepted them without attempting to change any of the conditions of the offer. For example, on one occasion when a teacher did not approve of the amount of noise pupils were making, she told them that if they did not "quiet down" they would not have any "personal plan time after recess".[2] The pupils accepted this offer by keeping the noise at a level that was acceptable to the teacher, thereby retaining the opportunity to have personal plan time after recess.

In Chapter 7 it was noted that on various occasions the pupils initiated bargains that resulted in negotiations between them and their teachers. On other occasions the teachers refused to negotiate pupil-initiated bargains. These bargains were frequently initiated by the non-negotiable and the intermittently negotiable pupils. Brief analyses of some examples

Alternatives open to the teachers	Rewards	Punishments
Bargain No. 1 Give the pupil permission to go to the library on condition that he will finish his work when he returns. This is the choice the pupil wants the teacher to take. Refuse to give the pupil permission to go to the library. Instead, require the pupil to finish his work before he goes to the library.	No explicit reward was offered by any of the pupils involved in these situations. From the teachers' perspective, the reward for accepting the choices the pupils wanted was the continuation and/or the enhancement of congenial relations with the pupils.	The pupils did not explicitly state the punishments for the teachers if they did not respond to their requests in positive ways. However, having interviewed each of the teachers concerned in those situations it seems that each teacher thought of the following results of not complying with the pupils' requests: Continual denial of requests made by the pupils may result in the teacher having difficulty in getting the pupils to go along with the interactive roles and agendas he would like to see them pursue. In each of these situations, the teachers did not comply with the pupil's request. There was no negotiation.
Bargain No. 2 Compromise on her earlier position, which was to give the pupil a detention, and have him do multiplication tables. The compromise the pupil wanted was to have the detention cancelled on condition that he have the tables done before returning to school the next morning. Stay with her original decision to give the pupil a detention and to have him do multiplication tables at that time.		
Bargain No. 3 To exempt a certain pupil from following the agenda set up for all of the pupils. Specifically, to make up a work plan for the day, do a problem for the "think board", and become involved in a think game. Not to exempt this pupil from following this agenda.		

of this variety of bargain are given in Table 7. The differences between the types of reward and punishment at the disposal of the teacher and those at the disposal of the pupil, when interacting with each other, have been observed in various situations to be a significant factor affecting the nature of the lines of action that are pursued. At other times, the differences have not played an important part in determining the nature of the interactions that occur between the occupants of these two positions in the school organization.

Teacher-teacher bargains. As in teacher-pupil interactions, some of the offers teachers make to each other are accepted, others are rejected, and still others are neither accepted nor rejected. The following are examples of offers made, accepted, and considered to be bargains by at least one of the participants in the interactions. They were not parts of observed episodes of negotiation, nor were they instrumental in initiating such processes.

EXAMPLE 1

A bargain was observed taking place between teacher C and teacher D. Teacher C asked teacher D if she would exchange one of her field trip times with her. The exchange took place without any disagreement or ambiguity being experienced by either C or D.

EXAMPLE 2

The day before a field trip was to take place, teacher F was overheard asking teacher G if she would stay with the pupils who did not want to go on the field trip while she and the other teacher on the team went along on the trip. Teacher G agreed without further discussion. Teacher F said that if teacher G wanted to go, she could. But teacher G willingly went along with teacher F's original proposal for her to stay in the school with the pupils who did not want to go on the field trip.

EXAMPLE 3

In addition to teaching other subjects, teacher J was also doing physical education. This program included house-league sports. Another teacher offered to help with these activities. This offer was immediately accepted by teacher J.

The intricateness of these and similar bargains was indeed difficult to pin-point. An attempt was made to analyse them with respect to the basic bargain elements of rewards and punishments. Each of the above examples is further presented in Table 8 to illustrate how this analysis was carried out. The preconditions of negotiation not present in these interactions are that no disagreement or ambiguity existed and, consequently, the goal of seeking a solution to disagreement or ambiguity was not present.

In the following situation an offer made by a teacher to her colleagues was not explicitly accepted or rejected, nor was it negotiated over.

At a planning meeting of one of the teams of teachers, the possible ways of fitting a music program into the schedules were discussed. Teacher A offered to take "a group" and have them sing Christmas songs. She added that she could take such a group if the other teachers were satisfied to cancel the "youth groups" for the next three weeks. After this offer was made, one teacher commented: "We should figure out something." Another teacher said, while looking at teacher A: "That is one possibility." Teacher A did not repeat the offer and none of the other teachers mentioned it.

The interaction over the issue of a music program as given in this description did not involve negotiating with teacher A over her offer to take part in it, even though there was an apparent disagreement between this teacher's offer and what the other members of the team wanted. All of the preconditions of negotiation were present in this situation, except the goal of seeking a solution to the apparent disagreement.

Seeking and Giving Advice

During the observations, an actor was said to be explicitly seeking advice if he asked for help with a problem. Conversely, an actor was said to be giving advice if he was attempting to give help or guidance concerning a problem. The following are examples of expressions used in seeking advice:

Teacher from teacher
—What would you do with . . . ?
—I've done everything I can think of, but it's all no good. Any suggestions?

TABLE 8   Analysis of Non-Negotiated Bargains in Teacher-Teacher Interactions

	Alternatives open to other teacher(s)	Rewards	Punishments
Bargain No. 1	Teacher D could exchange field trip times with teacher C.	There was no explicit reward for teacher D. It may have been an intrinsic reward in that teacher D seemed happy to do this. During an informal interview she said that she could give no explicit reason for her willingness to do this.	There was no explicit punishment for teacher D if she did not exchange times with teacher C. But one may justifiably infer that incidents of this nature help to develop and maintain an in-group structure in team situations.
	Teacher D could have refused to exchange field trip times with teacher C.		
Bargain No. 2	Teacher G could accept teacher F's suggestion that she stay in the school with pupils who did not want to go on the field trip.	Teacher G would be able to let any of her pupils who wanted to make the field trip go along with the other teachers. At a later date it was observed that teachers G and H went on a field trip with the class while teacher F stayed behind with the pupils who did not want to go.	

	Teacher G could have disagreed with teacher F's suggestion that she stay in the school with the pupils who did not want to go on the trip.	If teacher G did not accept the offer, she, in her own words, "would have to take all her kids each time". This is undesirable, in that there are always some pupils who do not want to go. She claimed that she could not expect the other teachers on her team to supervise her pupils if she did not supervise theirs also.
Bargain No. 3	Teacher J could have accepted the other teacher's offer.	Teacher J would have someone to help him with the physical education program. This may have been an opportunity for teacher J to collect a debt from the other teacher.	Teacher J may be putting himself in debt to the other teacher.
	Teacher J could have refused to accept the other teacher's offer to help.	Teacher J would not be putting himself in debt to the other teacher.	The offer was made without any consequences stated for teacher J if he refused it. The fact is that teacher J saw the negative consequences of not having someone to help him.

Pupil from teacher
—I do not understand this . . .
—Is this okay, or should I . . . ?
—I don't get it.

The expressions used by teachers to give advice to pupils are frequently different from those they use to give advice to their colleagues. The former were often closely related to directives. Here are three examples:

—Check with someone else.
—Make sure you have everything done before you leave.
—I think you should change this around and see what happens.

In open interaction, however, the giving of advice to pupils was not synonymous with the giving of directives. The verbal interaction in these circumstances was observed to include the following and other similar remarks by teachers:

—Let's see if we can figure this out.
—What should we do next?
—Barry has a problem. Anyone got any suggestions to help him?

These examples of teachers giving advice to pupils closely resemble the following responses, which teachers gave to some of their colleagues who were seeking advice.

—I don't know what I would do. . . . Probably I would . . .
—Why don't you try . . . ? It works for me.
—We will have to discuss this again. . . .

To elaborate further on the processes of explicitly seeking and explicitly giving advice, and to show how they are frequently peripheral to negotiation, some examples of each will be presented and the preconditions of negotiation that are absent in each situation will be pin-pointed.

Advice in teacher-pupil interactions. Pupils were observed seeking advice from teachers by following different procedures. The two procedures most frequently used were going directly to the teacher and seeking help, and raising a hand above the head and waiting for the teacher to respond. For example, when a pupil did not understand a part of the mathematics assignment that he was involved in, he raised his hand and kept it up until he got the teacher's attention, and then he asked for help. On another occasion, a pupil went to the teacher with his project and inquired if he was proceeding the "right way". The teacher reacted positively to the pupil's efforts and gave him some suggestions concerning the activities he wanted him to do.

The teachers on all of the teams observed frequently gave the pupils advice without having received explicit requests for it. Such was the case when a teacher spent four or five minutes "lecturing" to the class concerning the "proper" way to go to the library. He extolled the virtues of walking quietly and spoke disparagingly of their running and their noisy behaviour, which he claimed frequently disturbed other pupils.

When the foregoing situations are analysed in relation to the preconditions of negotiation, it may be seen that the interactions cannot be described as negotiations because two of the preconditions were absent. There were no expressed disagreements or ambiguities in the interactions and none of the actors had the goal of seeking solutions to disagreements or ambiguities through the process of negotiation.

Advice in teacher-teacher interaction. On various occasions several of the teachers were observed seeking advice from colleagues concerning disciplinary problems with certain pupils. Such was the case when a teacher asked the other members of his team for suggestions on "how to relate to Howard". Different approaches to teaching and to certain subjects were also topics on which teachers occasionally sought the advice of colleagues. Advice was explicitly sought when new situations arose. For example, a teacher sought the advice of other teachers on her team about a field trip on which she was going with her class. She asked whether it would be better to take the pupils before lunch and not come back until after lunch, or confine the trip to the morning or the afternoon. The two teachers who responded to this inquiry gave different opinions. One suggested it would be okay to stay over the lunch break, "if you have lots planned for them to do".

The other said she would not consider having the pupils out for that length of time because it would be "too difficult to keep them in line". In addition to giving advice when it was sought, many of the teachers on all of the teams observed volunteered advice to their team-mates at one time or another. For example, having watched teacher G test some of her pupils' reading abilities, teacher F made some suggestions to her. Teacher G indicated her appreciation of teacher F's comments by implementing some of the ideas they contained.

There were no expressed disagreements or ambiguities in many of the situations of giving and seeking advice in teacher-teacher interactions. Where disagreements and/or ambiguities did exist there was no attempt to solve them through negotiation.

General Discussions

"Discussion" is used to refer to situations in which actors have talked about problems or areas of concern and in some cases have made decisions about them. The actors in these situations did not see their interactions as negotiations. One teacher explained it by saying: "We just share our ideas and come to a mutual understanding." These interactions cannot be categorized as negotiations from an objective viewpoint because one or more of the preconditions of negotiation have been absent from each situation. Either both disagreements and ambiguities were absent from the situation, or the actors made no attempt to reach a collective agreement when they experienced one or both of these conditions. Discussions that have not been a part of any negotiations have often been observed in teacher-teacher interactions. Such discussions have been observed both in planning meetings and during less formal gatherings of teachers. Discussions also form an essential part of the teacher-pupil interactions in both formal and informal settings. A couple of examples from both the teacher-pupil and teacher-teacher interactions will illustrate that these discussions are often on the periphery of negotiation.

Teacher-pupil discussions. Many discussions were observed that involved both teacher and pupil, in learning situations, both in classrooms and in open-plan areas. Relatively few of

these discussions were parts of the observed episodes of negotiation. The discussions included both private and public situations. The former occur when a teacher gives individualized
attention to some pupils without other pupils observing the
interactions. Public discussions take place when pupils other
than those directly involved in the discussion are observing it.

Sometimes teachers attempt to get several pupils or even
the entire class to focus their attention on a discussion. For example, many teachers were observed holding "class meetings".[3] In these meetings the pupils were either active
participants or passive observers. On one occasion a teacher
and a group of approximately twenty pupils were discussing
the topic, "Rules for a Meeting". When not expressing their
views on this topic verbally, the pupils were expected to be attentive of what was being said. They were alternately actors
and audiences. To elaborate on the interactions in this situation we see that while the teacher was attempting to get the
pupils to develop the rules that should be followed at a meeting, the ideas expressed by the pupils were not always
congruent with those expressed by the teacher. The pupils,
however, did not resist modifying their ideas. For example,
some of the rules pupils proposed expressed similar ideas as
those given earlier by other pupils, leading the teacher and
the pupils to discuss the fact that the two rules expressed similar ideas and to come to an agreement about it without
negotiating their interactive roles and/or agendas. At another
point in this same situation, the teacher questioned the way one
of the pupils had stated a rule. He had stated it thus: "Keep
your mouth shut when someone else is talking." After a brief
comment, the teacher suggested other ways to state the same
idea, for example, "Be silent while others are talking," and
"Do not interrupt someone else."

Other discussions at class meetings covered a wide range of
topics, some of them suggested by pupils and some by the
teacher. These meetings were part of the teacher's over-all
plan to get the pupils thinking about and in some cases changing their ideas and plans of action, but the interactions in
them were frequently peripheral to negotiations, in that the
actors seldom saw their goals as being attainable through ne-

gotiation. In many of these situations the goals were achieved without disagreement or ambiguity, but in some situations these conditions prevailed and the actors attempted to alleviate them; hence the discussions became a part of the negotiation process. Whether negotiation took place or not, the empirical boundaries between discussion and seeking and giving advice were often indiscernible. Pupils frequently sought advice on academic and social problems they encountered. In the process of giving advice to these pupils, a teacher would simultaneously express ideas and attempt to get the pupils to volunteer their ideas and to make a decision about how to solve the problem.

Teacher-teacher discussions. The following example of teacher-teacher discussion did not involve negotiation. It took place at a meeting where teachers were planning a Christmas party for their classes. The party was to be held during regular school time, from 1:30 to 3:30 on the day before the school was to close for the Christmas break. There were four issues that they had to settle: (a) whether each class would have its own party or the three classes would be together for the occasion; (b) the way the games were to be organized, that is, how a pupil would know what game he was to play, when, and where; (c) the length of time the pupils were to spend at each game; and (d) when the pupils were to receive the "candy walking sticks"—before, during, or after the games. After brief comments by two of the teachers, who stated their reasons for wanting one party for the three classes, it was unanimously agreed that they would do this. When the teachers expressed their ideas on how the games should be organized, it was obvious that teacher F's ideas were not congruent with those of the other teachers; hence, one of the preconditions of negotiation was present in the interaction. Teacher F, however, accepted the opinion of the other teachers without any reservations. In other words, there was no negotiation to get anything changed or accepted. Since there was no resistance to certain courses of action, even though it was different from the expressed ideas of at least one of the actors, negotiation did not take place. Apparently, acceptance of the course of action suggested by other actors was seen by teacher F as more acceptable than negotiating over the differences between the courses of action outlined by the various actors.

Some discussions take place without a disagreement or ambiguity, and hence with no desire on the part of any of the participants to have other actors' ideas or behaviour patterns changed with respect to the issues discussed. For example, during a planning meeting of one of the teams observed, the five team members discussed their dissatisfaction with the way the music teacher was treating their pupils.[4] All of the teachers were, to a greater or lesser degree, upset about the music teacher's "unpredictable moodiness". Each teacher related incidents of behaviour that they classified as "undesirable" for a colleague to enact. One of the teachers asked what the others thought should be done about this situation, but no one gave any specific answer or suggestion. They only related their grievances concerning the music teacher's relationship with their pupils and with them as teachers. There was complete agreement on their expressed attitudes towards the music teacher; hence no actor expressed the goal of having all or part of her ideas concerning the music teacher accepted by the members of her team. The discussion seemed to serve the function of confirming and supporting the teachers' attitudes. All of the actors experienced some ambiguity over what was expected of them by a third party who was not present at the meeting. At this meeting the teachers did not attempt to focus a solution to this ambiguity. The plan of action necessary to correct the relationship between the music teacher and the pupils, as well as that between her and the other teachers, became the subject of an episode of negotiation that was observed at a later planning meeting.

Another category of interaction that is empirically interrelated to, and often a part of, each of the foregoing categories is one that may be labelled "Questions and Answers". This category was, on different occasions, observed to be separate from and yet a part of some of the categories discussed above, as well as of the interactions involved in negotiation. Therefore, in order to illuminate further the empirical boundaries of negotiation, it is deemed appropriate to note briefly the activities in this category in relation to the preconditions of negotiation.

Questions and Answers

It is a truism for teachers that questions play an important role in their teaching. The teacher, as Aschner (1961) notes, is "a professional question maker". Moreover, Aschner also claims that asking questions is "one of the best ways by which the teacher stimulates student thinking and learning". Asking questions of the class as a whole and of individual pupils was observed to be commonplace in the teacher-pupil interactions analysed in this research.[5] The teacher-teacher interactions were also observed to be frequently sustained by questions and answers. Interactions that involved only questions and answers were never observed to have all the preconditions of negotiation. There were always two or more actors present and both disagreements and ambiguities usually existed in the interactions. When the actors attempted to solve the disagreements and ambiguities, their verbal interactions involved more than the asking and answering of questions. In fact, various combinations of the above categories of activities were implemented. Even though there was a relatively small number of episodes of negotiation in comparison to the number of questions and answers in the interactions observed, the isolation of interactions that consist only of questions and answers helped to identify the empirical boundaries of negotiation.

Some categories of interaction were observed only in teacher-pupil interactions. It is to these categories that this analysis now turns.

TEACHER-PUPIL INTERACTIONS

In teacher-pupil interactions, teachers were observed giving orders to pupils and pupils were observed abandoning the role expectations teachers had for them. While the existence of one of these courses of action often meant that the other had been or would be implemented, the two courses also occurred independently of each other. On various occasions each category was observed to be part of a different episode of negotiation. Hence, the empirical boundaries of negotiation in teacher-pupil interactions were further illuminated.

Giving Orders

The orders given by the teachers were related to the framework of academic performance and disciplinary procedure.

While the orders in these areas were frequently accompanied by compliance on the part of the pupils concerned, the teachers did not always get the results they desired from such orders. Orders are frequently intertwined with other interaction strategies, such as bargains in which the positive aspects of obeying and the negative aspects of disobeying are more or less explicitly given. For example, a teacher who did not approve of the amount of noise among the pupils told them to "quiet down". To this she added that if they did not obey her they would not have any "personal-plan time after recess". This threat was used because many of the pupils liked the personal-plan times. In fact, the combination of an order and a bargain was successful in that it was accepted by the pupils without any attempt on their part to negotiate with the teacher.

One of the teachers observed had developed a unique and frequently effective method of getting the pupils to reduce their talking and moving around in the class area. When she wanted the noise level to be reduced she raised a hand above her head. After one or two of the pupils had seen what she was doing her message was quickly communicated to the other members of the class. The noise level usually dropped without the teacher having to give a verbal order or make any other body movements. Most teachers, however, give orders to their pupils verbally. The verbal orders observed during this research include:

—Be quiet.
—This work must be done by Thursday.
—If you cannot be quiet, Ralph, I will have to put you in the corridor to work by yourself.
—I am sorry but there is just too much noise here.
—You are much too fussy this morning.[6] If you do not change I will give you (specific activities) to do.

—Clean up the mess before you leave.
—Everybody must have this finished before he leaves.

In addition to being an impetus for negotiations, the giving of orders by teachers to pupils has been observed to be the cause of discussions and role abandonments that were not a part of any episode of negotiation. In many situations where orders had been given, the actors did not experience any disagreements or ambiguities. Also, on other occasions where disagreements did exist, teachers were observed refusing to negotiate with the pupils.

Role Abandonment

There are two types of role abandonment. One occurs when a pupil performs only the preliminaries to the role expectations. He accepts the social identity by attending class, but he does not embrace the role. For example, he refuses to listen attentively, to take notes, or to do any of the work expected of him. Only an occasional pupil acts in this way and then only on rare occasions. Such behaviour was uncommon among the pupils observed during this research. The most common type of role abandonment behaviour is when a pupil performs part of the over-all role expectations and then abandons the role, only to return to it of his own accord or after he has had some interaction with a teacher, or at least has been observed by a teacher.

Role abandonment is sometimes enacted as a strategy by pupils in their attempts to negotiate with teachers. An analysis of other examples of role abandonment revealed, however, that they were not enacted as strategies in the negotiation process. In fact, the reason for this activity is often difficult and sometimes impossible to ascertain. One reason isolated during an earlier study (Martin, 1970a:72-5) is the attempts of teachers to force pupils to comply with some role or to complete work that has been assigned to them. In attempting to get compliance, teachers often gave orders and illuminated the negative consequences of disobeying. For some pupils, the teachers had fairly reliable information on the possible reasons why they abandoned the role expectations held for them and became involved in extraneous activities. When other pupils abandoned the role expectations held for pupils in general, teachers could only speculate on the reasons for their "hopping out". But even the teacher was often bewildered by pupils' inattentiveness and lack of motivation.

A couple of examples of the enactment of role abandonment will further illustrate the empirical boundaries of this concept. One example of role abandonment was enacted by Leon during a poetry lesson. Instead of sitting, listening, and taking part in the discussions, he was observed walking around and appearing inattentive on four different occasions. After the class he said he was not "with it" during the poetry lesson. When questioned concerning Leon's inattentiveness, the teacher said he knew that Leon gets "turned off". He added: "He is like that almost all the time." Concerning another pupil who abandoned the over-all expectations and did not follow the agenda set out for him, the teacher commented that the pupil had to be left alone— "sometimes he tunes in, at other times he does not". In both of these situations there were discrepancies between the teacher's over-all role expectations concerning the agendas of the pupils and the activities the pupils were involved in, but negotiation did not take place because none of the actors in either situation attempted to change the other's opinions or courses of action. The pupils did not attempt to change the teacher's views of what their agendas should be. On various occasions, the teacher had apparently tried without success "to reach" these two pupils, but in the two situations reported on they did not make any explicit attempt to do so.

Having analysed some episodes of negotiation observed in teacher-teacher and teacher-pupil interactions, we have further delineated the empirical boundaries of negotiation by giving examples from each of the categories of social interaction that were observed on different occasions to be peripheral to and a part of negotiations. The type of data collected and the methods of analysis used in this study have been referred to as "soft", but the researcher has a strong emotional reaction in favour of becoming involved in the "bedrock reality" of social interaction as a prerequisite to analysing it. Therefore, the data have been experienced as having a "hard" quality that was found to be most productive in the effort to build back to more abstract formulations—hence, towards a theory of negotiation. The data also have implications relevant to teachers. Chapter 9 will be devoted to isolating specific aspects of a theory of negotiation, to pointing out the practical implications of the findings, and to stating the weaknesses and strengths of negotiation perspective.

1. It should be noted, for purposes of clarity, that while each of the categories has been discussed separately, the empirical boundaries of each are extremely difficult, and on occasion perhaps impossible, to locate. In fact, various combinations of the categories have been observed in the interactions in the school.

2. "Personal-plan time" is a time when pupils, in the words of one teacher, "may do as they please". Pupils must, in fact, stay in their own areas of the school and may choose from a variety of activities that the teacher deems appropriate for the occasion. These activities frequently include games, reading, and working on unfinished projects.

3. The idea of "class meetings" refers to situations in which the entire class is given an opportunity to discuss problems that have arisen. One teacher said that they provide an opportunity to discuss the "things which are important to us as a class".

4. The music teacher came to the classes of the teachers on this team on a number of occasions. She also had some of the children from the classes go to the music room at certain times on three days each week.

5. The nature of this research did not necessitate recording the frequency of questions in teacher-pupil or teacher-teacher interactions, but it is interesting to note that investigations have found a high frequency in the use of questions by teachers. For example, Floyd (1960) reported that ten primary-grade teachers asked an average of 348 questions each during a school day; Moyer (1965) found that twelve elementary-school teachers asked an average of 180 questions each in a science lesson; and Schreiber (1967) found that fourteen fifth-grade teachers asked an average of sixty-four questions each in a thirty-minute social studies lesson. A discussion of the use of questions in teaching and a bibliography of related studies have been given by Gall (1970).

6. Having spoken this sentence, the teacher asked if any of the pupils knew what it meant. One of the pupils said that it meant they were too noisy. The teacher confirmed this meaning.

9

Implications: Theoretical and Practical

Two often interrelated aims of empirical research are: to advance theoretical development, and to gather data that have direct or indirect practical application. By way of summary and conclusion, this chapter will deal both with the development of a theory of negotiation and with the practical application of the data reported in this study.

TOWARDS A THEORY OF NEGOTIATION

The notion of "theory" in sociology has several connotations (see, e.g., Homans, 1964; Merton, 1957; 1967; Zetterberg, 1965). Our concern here is with theory that provides modes of conceptualizing aspects of the social world. There are two kinds of theory that may do this: formal, and substantive (Glaser and Strauss, 1967:32-5, *et passim*). Formal theory is theory developed for a formal or conceptual area of sociological inquiry, for example, formal organization, socialization, and negotiation. Substantive theory acts as a bridge between formal theory and the empirical world. In other words, substantive theory is used to connect certain theoretically assumed entities that cannot be directly observed in or measured with the more or less directly observable or measurable aspects of social life that are under investigation. As such, it may be seen as a stage in the development of formal theory in a given area. Since the levels of generality exist only in terms of degrees, the boundary between formal theory and substantive theory is not explicit. Nevertheless, analytically, the focus is usually on one or the other.

Both substantive theory and formal theory must be specific, in that the basic entities and the process posited are expressed with clarity and precision. Both may be written in various forms. For example, they may consist either of a set of well-codified law-like propositions or of a theoretical discussion from which propositions may be derived. Regardless of the form used, two basically different types of statements are involved in the construction of a theory. One type defines the concepts of the theory, while the other expresses the relationships between the concepts (Schrag, 1967:225). Concepts provide the vocabulary of the theory and identify the phenomena with which the theory is concerned.

The various elements of theory must be integrated with one another. The elements are categories, properties of categories, and propositions or a theoretical discussion from which propositions concerning relations between the categories and their properties may be drawn. The stages of analysis involved in theory-building must be logically connected to each other. It may happen that formal theory is generated without moving from one level of theory to another, that is, from substantive theory to formal theory. This is the exception rather than the rule. Glaser and Strauss (1967:90-1) have put it this way:

. . . it is possible to formulate formal theory directly. The core categories can emerge in the sociologist's mind from his reading, life experiences, research and scholarship. He may begin immediately to generate a formal theory by comparative analysis, without making any substantive formulations from one area; though before he is through, he will have many fledgling substantive theories in his memos from his comparisons of substantive areas.

The process of theory-building requires both a faithful reportorial depiction of instances of interactions, and analytical probing into their character as well as a pin-pointing of propositions. These processes involve a continuous interplay between data-collecting, coding, analysing, and the developing of substantive theory of the social phenomenon under investigation. The research reported on here attempted to accommodate purposefully these processes and the required interplay. The time has come to give the theoretical implications of the findings of this research. The intention in doing so, is to contribute to the development of a theory of the negotiation that takes place among unequals (that is, the occupants of different formal positions in an organization) and among equals (that is, those who occupy the same formal position in an organization).

Negotiating Interactive Roles and Agendas

A comprehensive theory of the negotiating of interactive roles and agendas by occupants of the same formal position and by occupants of formally different positions in any social organization would deal with such things as the circumstances that give rise to negotiations, the directions of the negotiations, the assumptions about negotiations from which the negotiators work, the factors that have an effect on the processes of the negotiations, the strategies employed, the stages in the negotiations, the temporal aspects involved, the outcome of the negotiations, and the way negotiation fits into the gamut of interactions that can take place between and among the actors. The conceptual framework of negotiation used in the research reported on in this book was designed to deal with some of these issues.

The literature on informal negotiation, prior to this research, was such that it was not deemed appropriate to test particular hypotheses systematically. There was a need for further conceptual and theoretical development before such an approach could be of any great benefit. The qualitative analysis of the data in this research gave rise to three categories of proposition: (a) propositions that were discovered in the field early in the research and became central to the study; (b) propositions that were discovered in the field but not early enough to become central to the analysis—there was not time to pin-point the operations to the same extent as with those of the first category; (c) propositions discovered after the data were gathered—these could only be used to help with the interpretation of the episodes of negotiation already collected.

The remainder of this section will be a theoretical discussion of the negotiating of interactive roles and agendas. Rather than confining this discussion to negotiations in the school setting, the intention is to generalize, from the findings in the school setting to negotiations between unequals and among equals in any organizational setting where the interactions are sustained for a considerable period of time. The accuracy of the assumptions about the possibilities for generalizing the theory will be determined only by extensive research in a diversity of organizational settings.

Open and closed negotiations. Negotiations concerning interactive roles and agendas are a part of the interactions among equals, and they are also, frequently, important processes in the interactions among unequals. Given the findings in this research, it is reasonable to hypothesize that one of the major variables in negotiations involving the different types of actors is that negotiations between equals are more often of the open variety than those between unequals. Open negotiations occur in situations in which neither of the negotiators gives explicitly stated directives or consequences of not following a particular course of action. This is in contrast to closed negotiations, in which directives and consequences of not following them are explicitly stated by at least one of the negotiators. If the negotiator who is not in a position of authority gives explicit directives with or without consequences of not following them, the occupant of the authority position will often reciprocate with explicitly stated directives and consequences. On the other hand, the occupants of authority positions sometimes give explicitly stated directives and consequences of not following them to their subordinates, who do not state explicit directives in retaliation.

Since both open and closed negotiations take place between occupants of the same formal position in an organization, as well as between occupants of different formal positions, it may be seen that compatibility of perspectives and authority relations are alternate bases for social organization. Compatibility of perspectives implies an agreement on goals and means, while authority relations refer to the enforcement of particular courses of action by using the power associated with one's formal position in the social organization. Compatibility of perspectives is the primary basis for cohesion in teacher-teacher interactions in team situations in which effective sanctions through authority are absent. Compatibility may also be of significant importance in teacher-pupil interactions, but in these interactions the authority relation is waiting to be explicitly evoked if this is deemed necessary by the teacher.

Even though open negotiations are more prevalent in interactions between equals than in interactions between unequals, negotiations between equals may, on occasion, become closed and may even disappear from the interactions that take place. While closed negotiations are less frequent in interactions between equals than they are in interactions between unequals, it is worthy of note that they do occur. Two questions that merit further research, concerning the existence of closed negotiations between equals, are suggested by the fact that equals, by definition, have the same legal authority in the formal organization: Under what conditions do negotiations between equals become closed, and under what conditions is negotiation absent from the interactions between equals in the formal organization? Since the conditions that lead to closed negotiations frequently lead also to the termination of negotiations, it is appropriate to discuss simultaneously the conditions that, according to this research, may lead to either of these situations. When actors have the feeling that they are continually giving more to the interaction than they are getting from it, they may attempt to keep their interactions with those concerned to a minimum. If others continually fail to reciprocate, those who feel they are giving more than they are getting will refuse to negotiate. Intricately interrelated with the feeling of giving without receiving is the attitude that the primary group relations are inoperative for the actors concerned.

If occupants of the same position attempt to close an episode of negotiation, alternatives to negotiation will probably be more enticing to those they are attempting to force into compliance with their proposals. That is, if rewards and/or punishments are continually being explicitly stated in the interactions among equals, the conditions conducive to continued negotiations will not exist among them. Negotiation is seen as the more acceptable way of dealing with disagreements and ambiguities where there is an in-group structure. The development and healthy functioning of an in-group structure requires tactful handling of disagreements, ambiguities, and strategies in the negotiation process. Hence, the bluntness of explicitly stated directives and the consequences of not following them often militate against continuity of negotiations.

Power and leadership. Theoretically, teachers derive sufficient power from the legal structure of the school and from their expertise to have their pupils behave in ways they deem conducive to academic and social development. New teachers are apt to exert their authority to impose their own social order on the pupils, whereas more seasoned teachers are often reluctant to attempt to establish their own social order in their interactions with their pupils. However, there are times when all teachers will tend to terminate negotiations with their pupils. To generalize from the school setting to other settings, one can say that, whether the negotiation in the interactions between unequals is open or closed, if the person with legal authority views an episode of negotiation as being unsuccessful, he will tend to terminate it. Termination refers to a situation in which the negotiator with the highest authority is not willing to discuss an issue any further. It is the point at which he gives orders that a certain proposal must be carried out. The consequences of not performing the activities set forth in the proposal are also explicit. Although those in higher positions of authority use their authority to terminate negotiations, the interactions across status boundaries involve both crucial and trivial negotiations.

Crucial negotiations between unequals occur in situations in which the potential partisans have the possibility of exerting a fair degree of influence on the originator of the negotiations. The subject is important to the potential partisans, and either it is not so important to the originator (consequently, the potential partisans are able to gain through negotiations), or it is important to the originator but the potential partisans are, for other reasons, able to negotiate successfully with them. In both situations, a substantial change is likely to occur. Trivial negotiations, on the other hand, refer to situations in which power is firmly in the hands of one party, and the subject is important to that party. The potential partisans realize this, but they still attempt to influence the decision. In such situations there is not likely to be much change. If the potential partisans persist, they may force changes, but these changes will tend to be formal rather than substantive.

Theoretically, each occupant of the same formal position has the same potential ability to exert influence on each of the other occupant's decisions concerning the actions of all of the occupants of the position. If this were so, then the negotiations among equals would, for the most part, be of the crucial variety. But, in actuality, the negotiations between equals, like those between unequals, are often of the trivial variety. The significance of trivial negotiations lies in the fact that they often reaffirm the boundaries of interactive roles and agendas, especially after a disturbance.

The influence that the occupants of the same formal position have in relation to each other is usually derived from their acknowledged expertise and interaction tactics. While some teachers in team settings attempt to create continuous power-dependence relations, only a few attempt to monopolize leadership positions. The reasons for the reluctance of teachers in team set-ups to use their power in interacting with each other can only be speculated upon at this time. Power, as an influencing process in the interactions among the occupants of the same position in an organization, is of a precarious nature, especially where there is a diversity of expertise. Hence, each actor as a power-holder realizes that a colleague may soon become the power-holder. In other words, even though two actors occupy the same position in a formal organization, they may have varying degrees of power over each other. In addition, while one actor (A) may have more power over another actor (B) than B has over A in a given situation, the reverse could be true for another situation involving these two actors. Nevertheless, in these negotiations among equals, leaders do emerge and they do influence, to a greater or lesser degree, the activities of their colleagues. These leaders may be described as sporadic leaders and prevalent leaders.

Sporadic leaders, by definition, are those who are leaders on relatively few occasions. Their leadership, when it becomes active, may be derived from their recognized expertise on the issue being discussed and/or their successful enactment of persuasive interaction tactics at the time. On the other hand, prevalent leaders are leaders more frequently than their sporadic counterparts. The leadership of prevalent leaders spans many situations, and this may be due to these leaders' acknowledged expertise on the issues being discussed or negotiated over and/or to their greater skill in using the interaction strategies necessary to influence their colleagues in a variety of situations. Some of the negotiators do not have the recognized expertise in interaction strategies to become either prevalent leaders or sporadic leaders in any of the negotiation situations. They have only a minimum of influence on the decisions of leaders in the different situations. Hence, negotiations initiated by those who do not have recognized expertise or interaction skill will often be of the trivial variety.

Definition of others.   One actor's reactions to another actor are frequently constant across various types of situation. There is much evidence to suggest that individuals classify those with whom they interact. With regard to negotiations, the classification scheme specifies non-negotiables, intermittently negotiables, and continuously negotiables. This classification becomes established in the course of interactions between occupants of the same formal position as well as in interactions between occupants of different formally acknowledged positions in an organizational hierarchy. The data reported in this research reveal, however, that this kind of classifying is more prevalent in interactions between unequals than it is in interactions between equals. There are three significant processes that affect one's definition of others as belonging to one of the three categories. These processes become important because of their effect on subsequent negotiations. These processes include a self-fulfilling prophecy, accepting definitions of certain actors as given by others, and using indirect information to define others before or during one's interactions with them. To elucidate these processes, illustrations from the school setting will be used. Even though these examples are from only one type of organizational setting, it is postulated that the processes are not uncommon in other formal organizational settings or in other day-to-day interactions. Their general usefulness in explaining social interaction is worthy of analysis.

One aspect of the self-fulfilling prophecy in the school setting is the fact that teachers have expectations of their classes as a whole, as well as of individual pupils. Teachers generally expect that in any "ordinary" class of thirty pupils there are going to be three or four who will be industrious and "all-around-really-good-students". They also expect to have approximately an equal number of pupils who are unmotivated and lack discipline. The majority will be between the two extremes, and they make up the intermittently negotiable group. Another thing that seems to affect teachers' negotiations with pupils, and is not unrelated to the idea of self-fulfilling prophecy, is the fact that teachers often have expectations of pupils because of information they have obtained in indirect ways. For example, at one point in our observations a teacher said that one of her pupils was behaving in a similar way to his brother, who was "a discipline problem" when he was in the same school. The teacher did not have the brother in any of her classes, but she had heard of him. The information this teacher received in an indirect way about a brother of one of her pupils was used in developing predispositions concerning this pupil and hence affected her behaviour towards him.

The data also reveal that teachers sometimes rely heavily on other teachers' definitions of pupils. When a pupil moves from one class to another or from one area to another, word is passed on concerning his behaviour and his academic record. In extreme instances, that is, in the case of the "extremely bright student" or the "extremely slow learner", as well as in the case of the students who are classified as "discipline problems" in the school, the teachers "know the students" without having any personal contact with them. Teachers also have reputations which precede them.

The data collected in this research suggest the importance of these factors and indicate that further research on them would prove useful, not only for developing a theory of negotiation for the school but also for studying other areas of social interaction.

Negotiating strategies. Several strategies are employed in negotiating interactive roles and agendas in organizational settings. These include bargains, demonstrations, group pressures, comparisons, playing-off tactics, stalemates, and social-emotional strategies. A bargain is not a negotiation, but it may lead directly to a negotiation or it may be a strategy in an episode of negotiation already in progress. Bargains are exchanges between two or more parties. If an agreement cannot be reached concerning what is going to be exchanged, the parties involved may negotiate. Various bargains and a variety of interaction strategies may be combined in each episode of negotiation.

Demonstrations, in negotiations between unequals, occur when a negotiator who occupies a formally higher position in an organizational hierarchy behaves towards an individual or group of individuals in such a way as to demonstrate, to another individual or group, either the positive or the negative aspects of a certain kind of behaviour. In other words, a negotiator uses other individuals as demonstrators with the intention of influencing others to perform certain activities. The demonstrations used by equals when negotiating with each other are different from the demonstrations used in negotiations between unequals. Instead of using other individuals in negotiating with each other, equals pursue the courses of action which they want others to accept. The strategy is based on the rationale that others may be influenced to pursue certain courses of action if one demonstrates both his conviction to these courses of action and their value to the overall plan of action to be followed.

Group pressure refers to a group's attempts to induce changes in the attitudes and/or courses of action of an individual or another group. In negotiations between unequals, occupants of a formally higher position in a hierarchy may manoeuvre a situation so that it will be advantageous for some of the occupants of a lower position in the hierarchy to influence their peers to behave in certain ways. Unity among the occupants of the lower position may influence those in the higher position to follow specific courses of action. Hence, there are two varieties of group pressure. In one, pressure is applied within the group. In the other, a group unites and exerts pressure on someone outside the group to follow a particular course of action.

The strategy of comparisons is used when one actor compares another actor's behaviour towards him with the other actor's behaviour towards another person. That is to say, A compares B's actions towards him with B's actions towards C and judges them on the basis of their "fairness". This strategy is employed by pupils in negotiating with their teachers. Teachers have not been observed to use it in their interactions with pupils or with each other, hence the generalization that the strategy of comparisons is used more frequently by pupils than by teachers in teacher-pupil interactions. It may also be that this strategy is used more frequently by subordinates than by the superiors in most interactions in everyday life.

Playing-off is the process of playing one actor off against another. It has been observed that actors use this strategy in two ways: first, by intentionally and explicitly giving false information concerning the actions of other actors; and, second, by intentionally concealing the extent of one's information concerning the previous actions and desires of one or more actors. As with the strategy of comparisons, only pupils were observed enacting playing-off tactics. This does not mean that teachers never use this strategy. It does, however, suggest that pupils probably use it more often than teachers. Perhaps it is used more by subordinates than by superiors in all relationships.

Stalemates are employed only when a person is negotiating with someone occupying the same formal position in an organization. Stalemates may be resorted to intentionally by one or more of the negotiators or they may come about unintentionally. In stalemate situations, mediators are usually employed. The mediators may become involved by casually volunteering their services or they may be appointed by the negotiators. In fact, one of the negotiators may take on the role of mediator.

There are several theoretically possible outcomes of negoti-ations arising out of stalemates. Two were observed in teacher-teacher negotiations during the course of this re-search. In one case, negotiations were terminated because the negotiators, having commenced interactions with each other, experienced friction among themselves and were unable to continue the negotiations or initiate new episodes. In the other case, the stalemate was terminated and the negotiators were able to see some positive aspects in the results. Hence, they reinstated negotiation processes as a part of their in-teractions. Even if they did not interpret the results as having any positive aspects, the negotiators were not deterred, either by the results or by the interactions that led to them, from continuing to have what they considered to be meaningful in-teractions with each other. In such situations the stalemates actually served as cooling-off periods.

Social-emotional strategies include a wide range of activities that are, on different occasions, used by themselves or simul-taneously with other strategies. There are two interrelated varieties of this strategy. One emphasizes the negative aspects of emotional tactics, while the other emphasizes the positive aspects. Both varieties occur in negotiations between individ-uals of unequal status as well as between individuals of equal status. The desire to have others perform certain deeds some-times motivates a formally subordinate or superior actor to express a number of emotions. These expressions may be spontaneous emotional responses that are instrumental in eliciting favourable reactions from others.

The strategies used in negotiations between unequals and those used in negotiations between equals are sometimes dif-ferent. In negotiations between unequals, the occupants of one of the positions have at least some degree of authority over the occupants of the other position. On the other hand, compatibility of perspectives regarding goals and plans of ac-tion to achieve these goals is the primary basis for cohesion in

TABLE 9   Strategies in Negotiating Interactive Roles and Agendas

Strategies employed by occupants of the same formal
position when negotiating with each other

    Bargains
    Group pressures
    Social-emotional
    Demonstrations
    Stalemates

Strategies employed in negotiating with one's superiors

    Bargains
    Group pressures
    Social-emotional
    Comparisons
    Playing-off

Strategies employed in negotiating with one's
subordinates

    Bargains
    Group pressures
    Social-emotional
    Demonstrations

situations in which effective sanctions by authority are absent. In these interactions, threats to the compatibility of perspectives are usually taken seriously. The categories of strategy analysed in this study are summarized in Table 9. While generalizations have been presented concerning these strategies, the extent to which they are used in negotiations in other formal organizational settings, and in other day-to-day negotiations, can only be determined by further research.

Stages of negotiations.   While the specific interactions in negotiations are apt to vary from one episode of negotiation to another, the stages of negotiation between equals as well as those between unequals may be seen to follow a general pattern. The data of this research indicate that the following sequence is usually evident in teacher-pupil and in teacher-teacher negotiations: (a) stating the goals; (b) defining and redefining the situation; (c) using specific strategies (e.g., displaying one's bargaining counters and evaluating those of others, and enacting social-emotional, comparison, group pressure, and playing-off strategies); (d) re-evaluating the other's position to see if what was done in the earlier stages worked; (e) reaching a working agreement; and (f) solemnizing the agreement through implementation. This sequence of stages is absent from negotiations between unequals when the occupant of the higher position attempts to terminate it. The presence or absence of each of these stages helps to indicate the nature of the interactions taking place in a given situation.

To summarize, this discussion has generalized from specific findings in teacher-pupil and teacher-teacher negotiations to negotiations that take place in other organizational settings. There are several characteristics that are frequently found in the negotiations between unequals. Some of these are unique to situations in which the occupant of the highest formal position categorizes the other negotiators as intermittently negotiables. These characteristics include: (a) explicitly stated consequences for those who do not accept explicitly stated proposals, (b) a repetition of proposals and consequences, (c) recurring conflicts over the same issues, and (d) the relatively frequent use of authority. Other characteristics are common to the negotiations involving either the intermittently negotiables or the continuously negotiables. They include the following:

1. The period of time for which the negotiator who occupies the formally higher position assumes the working agreement will stand is frequently interrupted. These interruptions are more frequent in negotiations involving intermittently negotiables.

2. The negotiating time is shorter than that involved in the negotiations among equals.

3. The negotiations are of both the trivial and the crucial types.

4. Closed negotiation is enacted more frequently than open negotiation, but open negotiation appears more often in interactions with the continuously negotiables than in those with the intermittently negotiables.

5. There is frequently a reluctance on the part of the occupant of a superior position to make explicit use of his legal

authority in negotiating with occupants of a subordinate position. This reluctance is more frequent when the subordinate is defined as continuously negotiable than when he is defined as intermittently negotiable.

6. Bargains, demonstrations, group pressures, comparisons, playing-off, and social-emotional strategies are used in the negotiation process.

In contrast to the characteristics of negotiations between unequals, the following are common characteristics of negotiations between occupants of the same formal position in an organization:

1. The period of time for which the agreement is to stand is usually explicitly stated and the working agreement usually stands for this time.

2. The negotiating time is longer than for negotiations between unequals.

3. There is a reluctance to use the total power one has acquired through expertise and interaction tactics, but sporadic and prevalent leaders do arise.

4. Bargains, demonstrations, postponements, and social-emotional strategies are used.

5. Trivial and crucial negotiations exist in equal proportions.

6. Open negotiation is more common than closed negotiation.

The theoretical implications of the data have been presented, by moving towards a more general theory of negotiation, and it is appropriate now to isolate the relevance of this study to teachers.

IMPLICATIONS FOR TEACHERS

One significant finding of this study is that there are many similarities in the interactions that take place in different types of school. In fact, one of the greatest differences between open schools and closed schools may be in the architecture and not in the social interactions that take place. Open interaction as measured by negotiation, as well as individu-alized programs and flexible schedules, may be found in both closed- and open-plan areas. In short, the type of architecture does not necessarily indicate the nature of the teacher-pupil or the teacher-teacher interactions that take place in a school.

Our discussion of the development of a theory of negotia-tion indicates that there are often differences between teacher-pupil negotiations and teacher-teacher negotiations. These differences become apparent when one assumes the viewpoint of the teacher and seeks to determine the relevance of the findings for day-to-day interactions in the school. This discussion is divided into two parts, dealing with teacher-pupil interactions and teacher-teacher interactions.

Implications in Teacher-Pupil Interactions

There are two reasons why this study has significance for the practical aspects of teacher-pupil interactions. First, it reveals that teachers frequently categorize pupils as either non-nego-tiable, intermittently negotiable, or continuously negotiable. Second, it isolates the strategies teachers and pupils use to ne-gotiate with each other.

Teachers should ask themselves whether, intentionally or unintentionally, they categorize pupils on a negotiation con-tinuum. If so, according to what criteria? Which of the follow-ing criteria are used and what weight is given to each: performance, other teachers' definitions, demeanour and congeniality, clothing and appearance? Is the classifying of pupils simply a self-fulfilling prophecy in which the expecta-tion of finding certain types of pupils is met, if for no other reason than that the expectation is there?

Related to the issue of categorizing pupils is the question of the permanence of a category for a given pupil. Do pupils move from one category to another? If so, under what condi-tions does the move take place? The answers to these ques-tions, as communicated in teacher-pupil interactions, will be obvious indicators of the nature of the teaching being done in a given situation. For example, the significance of having pupils participate in the decision-making process of the interactions in learning situations, rather than attempting to impose a social order developed by the teachers, has been seen in a variety of situations.

It is often advantageous for individuals to have a knowledge of the strategies to be employed by each other in a given interaction. More specifically, it is to the teachers' advantage to be able to predict the strategies pupils are most likely to employ in the school setting. Conversely, pupils would find it to their advantage to know the strategies a teacher is likely to use in his interactions with them. In fact, learning the subtleties of interaction is one of the basic processes of socialization. It follows that isolating the strategies most often used by certain categories of actors when interacting with each other has far-reaching practical application to the socialization of individuals in general, and of individuals who are becoming members of certain formal organizations in particular; hence the practical value of isolating the strategies employed by pupils and teachers when interacting with each other.

Implications in Teacher-Teacher Interactions

In addition to isolating the interaction tactics used by teachers when interacting with each other, this study has pin-pointed some of the sources of conflict among teachers, as well as the actions that are generally helpful in reducing this conflict. Five major sources of conflict have been isolated:

1. Self-appointed leaders monopolizing their leadership roles.
2. The endeavour of officially appointed leaders to keep the asymmetrical relations between themselves and their subordinates conspicuous in all interactions.
3. The development of cliques based on such things as age, sex, philosophical orientation, and seniority.
4. Disagreements over disciplinary issues, for example, methods of discipline and the kinds of action to be considered acceptable in learning situations.
5. A belief that others are not doing their share of the work.

There are myriad ways in which conflict in teacher-teacher interaction may be reduced or eliminated altogether. The success of a particular course of action in reducing conflict in any situation is related to such factors as the frequency of interaction, the degree of the conflict, the temporal aspect of the conflict, and the anticipated frequency and nature of future interaction. All aspects of the broad career of the interaction, as well as all aspects of the interaction over the specific issue(s) on which there is conflict, may affect the success of a course of action aimed at reducing the conflict.

By using a framework of negotiation, this research has been able to isolate some of the predispositions and activities teachers have found to be important in their attempts at having "meaningful" interactions with each other. These predispositions and activities include, for example: taking in account the occupants of one's counter-identities, before getting involved in actions that might adversely affect them; being willing to assess one's merits and faults objectively and to use this assessment to create conditions conducive to open interactions; rotating the informal leadership role so that each teacher will have an opportunity to make use of his expertise; participating in the decision-making process as well as sharing responsibility for implementing the decisions made; implementing a cooling-off period when obstacles to open negotiation seem insurmountable; avoiding closed negotiations whenever possible; and terminating negotiations only after all legitimate courses of action have been explored. These observations could also be of use to principals who are attempting to keep their teaching teams intact.

Therefore, instruction in negotiation might advantageously be incorporated into the part of teacher training that is concerned with interpersonal dynamics, in the school in general, and in teacher-pupil and teacher-teacher interactions in particular. Teachers would thus be informed that negotiation may occur and in some instances should occur. Negotiation must be seen as a natural state of human interaction, even in schoolrooms. Hence, it is not to be stamped out but harnessed for the good of the aims of education.

Epilogue

The conceptual framework of negotiation as used in this study has several shortcomings. For example, in stressing the goal of reaching a collective agreement regarding the interactions when the action becomes problematic, it neglects to some extent the ultimate goals of the activities or their functions in the organization of which the actors are a part. The goals, other than those of reaching collective agreements, that make negotiations meaningful may need to be more adequately accommodated if we are to get a fuller understanding of the interactions that take place in an organizational setting. Probably the biggest weakness of this framework is that it encourages one to overlook the more stable aspects of social interaction. Other non-negotiable aspects of interaction are also only alluded to and are not analysed as such when one gives rigid adherence to this framework.

Offsetting these weaknesses, negotiation as a conceptual framework for analysing social interaction has three basic strengths. First, it may be noted that, by looking at social interaction as a process of interpreting and defining one another's acts, the framework is able to cover a wide range of human associations; for example, conflict, domination, exploitation, consensus, disagreement, indifferent concern for another, and closely knit identification. Secondly, although there may be a tendency in using this framework to explain social action by the way the individual participants interpret and define situations, the framework can handle intergroup interaction. Thirdly, the framework can handle both micro-level changes (that is, changes in the context of relatively short episodes of negotiation as analysed in this study) and macro-level changes (that is, large-scale institutional changes).

Appendix A

Questionnaire
Used in the Formal Interviewing
of School Principals

The data collected during the formal interviewing of principals were used in the process of selecting teaching teams for the formal interviewing of teachers and the observational phase of this research.

1. Type of economic area which the school serves.
   lower__ middle__ upper__ mixed__
2. Number of teachers in the school. __
3. Number of open areas. __
4. Number of classrooms. __
5. Do you have team teaching? Yes__ No__
   (Definition of team teaching: two or more teachers who share the responsibilities and functions of instructing a given group of pupils in one or more defined content areas; for example, mathematics, social studies, science, etc.)
6. How many teaching teams do you have in each of the following categories?
   a) In their first year of operation as a team__
   b) In their second year of operation as a team__
   c) In their third year of operation as a team__
   d) More than three years of operation as a team__

Appendix B

Questionnaire
Used in the Formal Interviewing
of Teachers

BIOGRAPHIC DATA

1. Male__ Female__
2. How many years have you taught in this school? __
3. Are you a member of a teaching team? Yes__ No__
   If yes, how many years have you worked with this team? __
4. How many years have you taught elsewhere,
   a) in a classroom? __
   b) in an open area? __
5. Do you hold a teaching certificate? Yes__ No__

INTERACTION DATA

6. a) How often are the following items discussed by the members
      of your team? Select one category from this card (Card 1) for
      each item I read to you.

      Card 1
      A = Never
      B = Rarely
      C = Sometimes
      D = Rather Often
      E = Frequently

   b) Are there other issues which are discussed by the members of
      your team at either planning meetings or other times in the
      school?
7. a) Who usually takes part in the discussions of the following

issues? (The issues given in question 6a as being discussed with a frequency of B, C, D, or E on card 1 were read out here.) Select your answer from this card (Card 2). You may need to select more than one category on this card, for example, B and E, or C and F. In other words, the category E (or F) may or may not appear with either one of the others.

Card 2 (used where teacher interviewed was on a team of five members)
B = All the teachers on the team
C = Only four of the teachers on the team
D = Only three of the teachers on the team
E = Only two of the teachers on the team
F = Others

Card 2 (used where teacher interviewed was on a team of four members)
B = All of the teachers on the team
C = Only three of the teachers on the team
D = Only two of the teachers on the team
E = Others

Card 2 (used where teacher interviewed was on a team of three members)
B = All of the teachers on the team
C = Only two of the teachers on the team
D = Others

b) Give each teacher on your team a number. Take number 1 for yourself and assign numbers 2, 3, 4, and 5 where necessary (that is, if there are four or five members on the team) to the other members of your team. Now, concerning the following issues, who do you think has the most influence in making the decisions? Answer by giving only one number UNLESS you are really convinced that more than one has equal influence. If someone from outside of the team has greater or equal influence in the decisions made on the team include the letter "O" with your response. You may use this card (Card 3) to help in the assigning of numbers to each team member and in giving your responses.

Card 3
Teacher 1 (myself)
Teacher 2
Teacher 3

Teacher 4

Teacher 5

Person outside the team "O"

The following is the list of items used in questions 6 and 7. This is also the form that was used to record the responses to these questions. Both of these questions were asked simultaneously. In other words, the expectation items were only read once, then the teacher was asked to give the frequency of the discussions, the participants in them, and the person(s) with the most influence.

	Items	Frequency (question 6a)	Participants (question 7a)	Influence (question 7b)
i)	Individualized instruction			
ii)	Grouping of students			
iii)	Maintenance of order in the classroom or open area			
iv)	Curriculum development			
v)	Following a time-table			
vi)	The amount of team teaching to be done			
vii)	Teaching methods to be used			
viii)	The part the pupils are to play in deciding what activities they are to do			
ix)	Methods of disciplining pupils			

	Items	Frequency (question 6a)	Participants (question 7a)	Influence (question 7b)
x)	Supervising pupils			
xi)	Scheduling activities			
xii)	Keeping records			
xiii)	Procedures for pupil evaluation			
xiv)	Experimentation in teaching and learning situations			
xv)	Your over-all relationship with pupils			
xvi)	Your over-all relationship with other teachers			
	Others (question 6b)			

8. I am interested in the ways you try to get other teachers on your team to change their minds and/or behaviour in the following situations:

   a) On decisions they have made or behaviours they have already carried out.

   list of things done   frequency (card 1)

   _____   _____

   _____   _____

   b) On decisions which you know they are going to make shortly and/or behaviours you think they are going to enact shortly.

   _____   _____

   _____   _____

c) In situations where you think there should be a decision made, but other teacher(s) do not think so.

_____   _____

_____   _____

9. a) With regard to aspects of your work at school, do you ever make decisions or enact behaviours which affect other teachers and which they do not always agree with? Yes___ No___

   b) If yes, I am interested in how you go about:

   i) Persuading teachers to go along with a decision you are about to make or to do the activities you would like to see done.

   list of things done   frequency (card 1)

   _____   _____

   _____   _____

   ii) Persuading teachers to abide by a decision you have already made or to follow your example in activities you are already doing.

   _____   _____

   _____   _____

10. I have a list of ways in which people go about attempting to influence others. Teachers, at one time or another, may do some, if not all of these things. I am interested in how often you do each of these things in attempting to get pupils and other teachers to change their minds on different issues and their activities on different occasions.

    a) For each item I read out please tell me how often you do it, first to pupils and then to teachers, by selecting the appropriate categories on this card (Card 1).

    b) I would also appreciate getting as many examples of each of these as you can recall from your experiences in the school situation.

The following is the list of categories used in this question; it is also the form that was used to record the responses of the teachers.

Categories of activities used to influence others	Frequency (Card 1)		Specific examples
	Pupils	*Teachers*	
i) bring them new information			
ii) remind them of your experience in teaching situations			
iii) keep your inter-action with them at a minimum			
iv) work through other teachers			
v) work through pupils			
vi) co-operate			
vii) flatter			
viii) show displeasure			
ix) refuse to co-operate			
x) pretend to be concerned when you are not			
xi) argue			
xii) make a joke out of a situation when everyone else thought the situation to be a serious one			
xiii) let your routine activities be the most important factor			
xiv) plead			
xv) promise			
xvi) others			

Appendix C

Guideline Questions

Guideline questions used during the informal interviews of the observational phase of the study.

STRATEGIES

1. Why do you do *(the specific behaviour observed)* ?
2. a) Did you try to influence Mr. X's behaviour or attitude during *(Here I gave either the specific time when I thought negotiation may have taken place or the issue which I thought was negotiated over.)*
      Yes _____   No _____
   b) If yes, what did you do?
   c) If no, why didn't you do something?

EXTENT
Direction

3. a) Who do you think had the most influence during *(the specific situation observed)*?
   b) What part did you play in this situation?
   c) How did you do this?

Intensity

4. a) Were you concerned about the outcome? Yes———— No————
   b) If no, why did you become involved in it?
   c) If yes, why were you concerned?

5. a) Do you think other team members were really concerned about the outcome? Yes——— No———
   b) If no, why weren't they?
   c) If yes, why were they?

OUTCOME

6. What was the outcome of the interactions in question? In other words, which one of the following things happened?
   a) One person's point of view got accepted in its entirety.
   b) All of the actors compromised.
   c) Nobody really compromised.
   d) Everyone seems to have won.
   e) If the above possibilities are inadequate to describe the results, give, in your own words, what you think they were.
7. Was the outcome effectively put into practice? (The answer to this question was sought after the relevant time had elapsed following the observed negotiation.)

Appendix D

Data Collected on the Forced-choice Questions of the Formal Interviews with Teachers

TABLE 10   Expectation Scores for Open and Closed Areas

	Scores Type of Area		Differences between
Expectation Items	Open	Closed	open and closed
Curriculum development	35	25	+ 10
Grouping of pupils	29	25	+ 4
Procedures for pupil evaluation	25	25	0
Individualized instruction	29	20	+ 9
Amount of team teaching to be done	24	22	+ 2
Experimentation in teaching	21	19	+ 2
Pupil participation	17	11	+ 6
Teaching methods	17	20	− 3
Maintenance of order	14	23	− 9
Scheduling of activities	11	21	− 10
Methods of discipline	16	15	+ 1
Keeping records	10	13	− 3
Supervising pupils	13	9	+ 4
Following a time-table	11	9	+ 2
Over-all relationship with the pupils	16	20	− 4
Over-all relationship with other teachers	9	17	− 8

TABLE 11 Influence Scores for Open and Closed Areas: Teachers' Perceptions of Their Using Different Plans of Action to Influence Their Counter-Identities

| | Type of Area | | | | | |
| | Open | | Closed | | Differences between open and closed in teacher-to-student scores | Differences between open and closed in teacher-to-teacher scores |
Plans of Action	teacher to teacher	teacher to student	teacher to teacher	teacher to student		
Co-operate	29	28	29	31	+ 3	0
Argue	28	11	17	18	+ 7	− 11
Let routine activities be the most important factor	20	20	21	14	− 6	+ 1
Bring new information to the situation	16	20	20	27	+ 7	+ 4
Flatter	14	24	20	31	+ 7	+ 6
Make a joke out of the situation when many of those in the situation thought it to be a serious situation	8	8	13	29	+ 21	+ 5
Show displeasure	10	20	10	32	+ 12	0
Pretend to be concerned when you are not	7	13	8	13	0	+ 1
Keep interaction at a minimum	7	9	6	11	+ 2	− 1
Work through other teachers	3	20	10	12	− 8	+ 7
Make promises	2	14	7	29	+ 15	+ 5
Remind others of one's experience in teaching situations	1	9	6	17	+ 8	+ 5
Refuse to co-operate	4	6	3	15	+ 9	− 1
Work through students	2	20	4	16	− 4	+ 2
Plead	2	7	4	14	+ 7	+ 2

Appendix E

Sample Episodes of Negotiation

Negotiation Episode 13

BACKGROUND INFORMATION

A teacher made an offer to her class, that each pupil who completed his work satisfactorily would be given permission to go on the next class project outside the school. She made the offer to the entire class, even though "most of the students do their work, anyway". When the time came for the next class trip, one pupil had three assignments that he had not finished. In line with her original offer, the teacher told this pupil that he could not go on the trip. Instead, he was to join the class of another teacher for the rest of the school day. He was to finish his assignments under the supervision of that teacher. The pupil had a strong desire to accompany his class-mates, so he attempted to negotiate with his teacher.

PRECONDITIONS

1. This was a situation, in which a pupil wanted to change the policy of the teacher. There was a disagreement, in that the pupil thought an exception should be made to the rule concerning who could go on the class trip, but the teacher did not think so.

2. The pupil wanted to negotiate with the teacher to be exempted from the bargain the teacher had offered the

pupils. The teacher did not want to negotiate over this issue. She wanted the offer to apply to everyone. Therefore, she thought that the reward should be withheld from those who did not comply with the ruling she had made.

EXTENT

Content Whether a pupil who had not complied with an offer should receive the reward which those who complied with it received. Should he receive this reward, just for once? Hence, both the interactive roles and the agendas of this pupil and teacher were negotiated in this situation. The interactive roles, however, seemed to be the most important issue at stake.

Direction A pupil initiated the negotiation with a teacher in order to get a favour.

Intensity The episode of negotiation turned out to be crucial, in that the pupil got the favour he sought. But he got this favour only after he had agreed to complete his work when the project outside of the school was over.

STAGES

1. When the pupil learned that he could not go on the field trip, he became "very upset", according to the teacher, and "almost cried". He said he would not go to the classroom, where he was to be supervised, while the rest of the class was on the field trip. The teacher, however, insisted that he go to that classroom. She said he did not do the work that had been assigned to him, and "he had to suffer the consequences." She reasoned that everyone else had followed her instructions and this particular pupil should also have done so. (This stage took place before noon and the trip was to take place at 1:30 p.m. on the same day.)

2. The pupil went to the teacher at lunch-time and said he would have all his work finished within a couple of days. At this time, according to the teacher, the pupil "pleaded" with her, and she told him that she would let him know after lunch.

3. When the time came for the class to leave on the trip and for the pupil who had not finished his assignments to go to another classroom to work on them, the teacher said that she took "pity" on him and decided to let him go along with the rest of the class. This permission came only after the pupil had "promised to have his work completed by next Monday".

STRATEGIES

1. The teacher attempted to stand firm on her demands, that is, on the bargain which she had made with the pupils.
2. The pupil "pleaded" with the teacher, and promised that he would finish his work after he had received the reward.

OUTCOME

1. The teacher compromised on her earlier plan of action.
2. The pupil was granted the privilege he sought, but in return he had to make a commitment for his agendas.

Negotiation Episode 14

BACKGROUND INFORMATION

This episode of negotiation was observed in a classroom. It started when a teacher was trying to find out who had which books from the library. It continued until the teacher had completed this task.

PRECONDITIONS

1. The teacher seemed to be speaking to the entire class, but an informal interview revealed that he was actually referring only to a few pupils. He said: "They knew who I meant."
2. This was a recurrent situation, in which different results were produced by similar interaction patterns. Sometimes the pupils got away with being "a little noisy". At other times they got punished for this. At the time of this episode there was a disagreement concerning the amount of noise in the class.
3. A number of the pupils had a collective goal, their plan of action being to continue to talk and move around in the classroom. The teacher's goal was to put an end to the

pupils' noisiness. He claimed that the noise was created by "unnecessary moving around" and "talking". His goal was to stop these activities altogether or at least to reduce them.

EXTENT

Content   The amount of "noise" to be tolerated by the teacher. The interactive roles of the existing situation and the agendas of future situations were being negotiated.

Direction   The pupils initiated the negotiation with the teacher.

Intensity   The subject-matter was important to the teacher and to the pupils. The potential partisans (the pupils) exerted a fair degree of influence on the authority (the teacher), and substantial changes came about in the teacher's plan of action. Hence, this episode may be classified as a crucial negotiation.

STAGES

1. The teacher told his class that they had to listen to him as he spoke to them concerning library books. He said he wanted all of the pupils to "pay attention" to what he was saying.
2. According to the teacher's definition of the situation, some of the pupils did not obey his request for their attention. The teacher noted that at first his telling the pupils to be quiet was "a request", but when they did not follow the request he turned it into "an order".
3. Some of the pupils continued to talk and move around.
4. Four or five minutes later, the teacher said: "Be quiet." He waited a few seconds, and then, as he looked around the room, he said: "A few people are still talking."
5. Shortly after this, the teacher said: "Okay, if you want to talk you'll have to stay after 3:30."
6. The teacher continued to inquire as to who had which books from the library. The pupils were quiet for a few moments, but, according to the teacher, became "noisy" again. He stopped his activity and said: "Some of you

should remember yesterday." [In an informal interview, the teacher noted that several of the pupils had had to stay in after 3:30 the day before for behaviour similar to that in the incident described here.]

7. The teacher continued to explain about the books. He was interrupted on various occasions by a couple of the pupils. To each of these pupils he said: "Raise your hand before you speak." After the teacher had finished talking about the library books, he put four names on the board for all to see. These four pupils had been given detentions.

STRATEGIES

1. The teacher used the following strategies: (a) He repeated the "suggestion" or "order" that the pupils are to listen while he was inquiring about the library books. (b) He threatened to keep the pupils in after 3:30 if they did not listen to him. (c) He reminded the pupils of their previous experiences. (d) He gave detentions to some pupils.
2. The pupils' strategy was to ignore the teacher's requests and orders and to continue to talk and move around.

OUTCOMES

1. Some of the pupils co-operated with the teacher and complied with his request.
2. Other pupils continued to enact the behaviour the teacher had asked them not to enact. They stopped enacting this behaviour only after the teacher threatened to give them detentions.
3. Some of the pupils continued to go against the wishes of the teacher, even after he had turned his "suggestion" into an "order". They continued this misbehaviour, despite a threat that they would be given detentions. In other words, the threat and the reminder of earlier punishments did not achieve the teacher's desired plan of action for all of his pupils.

Negotiation Episode 15

BACKGROUND INFORMATION

A teacher was testing a pupil's reading ability when the bell rang, indicating that it was time for a recess. She wanted to leave the teaching area during the break, but she did not want to tell the pupil this. Instead, she asked him if he wanted "to stay and finish" the test, or "leave and finish it after recess". To her surprise and dismay, the pupil said: "I want to finish it now." He also indicated that he would rather take a few minutes' break after the activity was completed than take it immediately and have to come back to reading after recess. The teacher did not accept this idea. Nor did she tell the pupil that he had to leave and come back after the recess. Instead, a brief negotiation was entered into.

PRECONDITIONS

1. This was a situation in which a teacher lacked knowledge of what a pupil's response would be to her question. In other words, there was a sort of ambiguity in the situation. Once the pupil had made his response, the teacher disagreed with it, but she attempted to make her disagreement not too obvious at first.
2. The teacher's goal was to reach an agreement with the pupil without forcing him to come to her terms. Because the pupil's response indicated "an interest" in the activity, she did not want to tell him to leave and come back later.

EXTENT

Content   The general guidelines for the agendas of both actors were being negotiated.

Direction   The pupil's response to the teacher's question was instrumental in starting the negotiation with the teacher.

Intensity   The issue was important to each actor. The pupil's decision to stay and finish his reading test was not carried out because of the teacher's negative reaction to it. Therefore, this negotiation may be classified as a trivial one.

STAGES

1. The teacher asked the pupil if he wanted to stay and finish the activity they were engaged in, or finish it after the break. The pupil indicated that he would rather stay and

finish his reading before taking his recess than have to return to it after the recess.

2. The teacher said the test would take the entire recess period. She added: "Probably you have things to do recess time." The pupil replied that he did not have anything to do. He suggested that he finish the reading test immediately and take a break later.

3. The teacher did not accept the pupil's offer to work immediately and take a break later. She rejected it in a very subtle way. She noted that it was "nice outside". After a brief pause she said: "I think it is better to wait until 10:45. Come back then and it will only take a few moments to finish."

4. Reluctantly, the pupil went outside for his recess.

STRATEGIES

1. The pupil made an offer to the teacher prior to the negotiation, and repeated it during the negotiation process.

2. The teacher implicitly and politely refused to go along with the pupil's suggestion. Even her final strategy (stage 3) did not take the form of an explicit directive for him to leave. Instead, she said: "Come back . . ." Thus she implied that he had to leave.

OUTCOME

The teacher did not compromise at all. Her desires concerning her own agenda and the agenda of the pupil were carried out at the expense of the pupil's original proposal.

Negotiation Episode 16

BACKGROUND INFORMATION

This negotiation took place during several informal meetings of the teachers on this team. Since not all of these meetings were observed, much of the data had to be obtained by informal interviews.

PRECONDITIONS

1. There were ambiguities in the situation, in that the teaching-team had not reached any decision regarding

what should be included in a particular subject area that they were dealing with as a team. In attempting to dispel the ambiguities, the actors encountered a disagreement among themselves.

2. All three of the actors involved in this negotiation viewed it as an episode of negotiation. One teacher thought that her idea of how to change the ambiguous situation was worth presenting to her colleagues. Having presented her proposal, she met with an unanimous rejection by her teammates. Their goal became to prevent this teacher's idea from being implemented.

EXTENT

Content   The pros and cons of including a certain topic in the general subject area of communication were presented. In addition to this issue, which may be classified under the rubric of agendas, the interactive roles of the actors were at stake.

Direction This may be indicated by noting that one teacher was negotiating against the two other members of her team. A coalition of two was negotiating against the third in this triadic situation.

Intensity This episode of negotiation has been classified as a trivial one, in that teacher F, the originator of the issue, did not compromise or in any way change her proposal. Her decision was carried out despite the opposition of the other members of the team.

STAGES

1. At a planning meeting, teacher F said she wanted a certain topic included as a section in their "communication tree". The other teachers disagreed. After discussing this issue for the last ten or fifteen minutes of the meeting at which it came to the fore and was first observed, the teachers had not reached an agreement. Teacher F gave her reasons for wanting to include the topic in a particular place, while the other teachers offered counter reasons for its exclusion.

2. The teachers pursued their haggling at various informal meetings during the day.

3. Two days later, teacher F reported to the researcher that the two other teachers had suggested that the topic she thought should be included in the "communication tree" should be included in other parts of their language program. Teacher F agreed, but said that it should also be included in the communication part.

4. The teachers reported discussing the issue at various times over a period of more than a week.

5. Finally, the two teachers who had opposed teacher F's original proposal said they could see the validity of her point and had decided to go along with her proposal. However, they repeated their contention that the topic could be included in other parts of their language program. Teacher F did not express any disagreement with this.

STRATEGIES

1. There were many discussions in which each side attempted to put the other on the defensive.

2. Two teachers attempted to get the third to compromise and put a topic she thought should be in the "communication tree" in another part of their program.

3. An unintentional cooling-off period seemed to play a key role in the final outcome.

OUTCOMES

1. Two teachers compromised, and one person's point of view was accepted in its entirety. The two saw themselves as behaving in a compromising way.

2. All of the actors later stated, separately, that they thought everyone had won.

References

AMIDON, E., and A. SIMON.
1965   "Teacher-pupil interaction". *Review of Educational Research* 35 (2): 130-9.

ANDERSON, D. C.
1970   "Open plan schools: time for a peek at Lady Godiva". *Education Canada* 10 (2): 3-6.

ANDERSON, H. H.
1939   "The measurement of domination and of socially integrative behavior in teachers' contact with children". *Child Development* 10 (2): 73-89.

ARGYLE, M.
1967   *The Psychology of Interpersonal Behavior.* London: Penguin Books.
1969   *Social Interaction.* Chicago: Aldine-Atherton.

ASCHNER, M. J.
1961   "Asking questions to trigger thinking". *National Education Association Journal* 50: 44-6.

BALES, R.
1950   *Interaction Process Analysis: a Method for the Study of Small Groups.* Cambridge, Massachusetts: Addison-Wesley.

BALINT, M.
1957   *The Doctor, His Patient, and the Illness.* New York: International Universities Press.

BARTON, A.
1968   "Hard soft". *School Progress* 37 (September): 54-6.

BECKER, H. S.
   1952   "Social-class variations in teacher-pupil relationships".
          Journal of Educational Sociology 25 (4): 451-65.

BEGGS, D. W. (ed.).
   1964   *Team Teaching: Bold New Venture*. Indianapolis: Unified
          College Press.

BENNIS, W. G., and H. A. SHEPARD.
   1961   "A theory of group development". Pp. 321-40 in W. G.
          Bennis, K. D. Benne, and R. Chin (eds.), *The Planning of
          Change*. New York: Holt, Rinehart and Winston.

BERNSTEIN, B.
   1967   "Open schools, open society?" *New Society* 10 (259).

BLAU, P. M.
   1964   *Exchange and Power in Social Life*. New York: Wiley.

BLUMER, H.
   1969   *Symbolic Interactionism: Perspective and Method*. Englewood
          Cliffs, New Jersey: Prentice-Hall.

BORAH, L. A., JR.
   1963   "The effects of threats in bargaining: critical and experi-
          mental analysis". *Journal of Abnormal and Social Psychology*
          63: 37-44.

BOYD, R.D., and M. V. DEVAULT.
   1966   "The observation and recording of behaviour". *Review of
          Educational Research* 36 (5): 529-50.

BRITTAN, A.
   1973   *Meanings and Situations*. London: Routledge & Kegan Paul.

BROWN, B. R.
   1968   "The effects of need to maintain face on interpersonal
          bargaining". *Journal of Experimental and Social Psychology* 4:
          107-22.

BROWNE, J.
   1973   *The Used-Car Game: a Sociology of the Bargain*. Lexington,
          Massachusetts: D. C. Heath.

BUCHER, R., and J. STELLING.
   1969   "Characteristics of professional organizations". *Journal of
          Health and Behaviour* 10 (March): 3-15.

BUNYAN, L.
   1967   "There's lots more to team teaching than the kind of build-
          ing you have". *School Progress* 36 (January): 72-6.

CALLAHAN, R. E.
   1962   *Education and the Cult of Efficiency*. Chicago: University of
          Chicago Press.

COGAN, M. L.
  1956 "Theory and design of a study of teacher-pupil interaction". *The Educational Review* 26 (4): 315-42.

COHEN, E. G.
  1973 "Open-space schools: the opportunity to become ambitious". *Sociology of Education* 46 (2): 143-61.

CORWIN, R. G.
  1965 *A Sociology of Education.* New York: Appleton-Century-Crofts.

DENZIN, N. K.
  1970 *The Research Act: a Theoretical Introduction to Sociological Methods.* Chicago: Aldine.

DEUTSCH, M.
  1958 "Trust and suspicion". *Journal of Conflict Resolution* 2: 265-279.

DEUTSCH, M., and R. M. KRAUSS.
  1960 "Effects of threat upon interpersonal bargaining". *Journal of Abnormal and Social Psychology* 61: 181-9.
  1962 "Studies of interpersonal bargaining". *Journal of Conflict Resolution* 6: 52-76.

DREEBEN, R.
  1970 *The Nature of Teaching.* Glenview, Illinois: Scott, Foresman.

FLANDERS, N. A.
  1951 "Personal-social anxiety as a factor in experimental learning situations". *Journal of Educational Research* 45 (October): 100-10.
  1965 *Teacher Influence, Pupil Attitudes, and Achievement.* United States Department of Health, Education and Welfare, Office of Education Cooperative. Research Monograph 12. Washington: Government Printing Office.
  1970 *Analyzing Teaching Behavior.* Reading, Massachusetts: Addison-Wesley.

FLOYD, W. D.
  1960 "An analysis of the oral questioning activity in selected Colorado primary classrooms", (Doctoral dissertation, Colorado State College.) Ann Arbor, Michigan: University Microfilm Number 60-6253.

FOOTE, N.
  1951 "Identification as the basis for a theory of motivation". *American Sociological Review* 16 (1): 14-21.

FREIDSON, E.
  1961 *Patients' Views of Medical Practice.* New York: Russell Sage Foundation.

FRENCH, J. R. P., JR., and B. H. RAVEN.

1958 "Legitimate power, coercive power and observability in social influence". *Sociometry* 21: 83-97.

1959 "The bases of social power". Pp. 118-49 in D. Cartwright (ed.), *Studies in Social Power*. Ann Arbor, Michigan: University of Michigan Press.

FUCHS, E.

1969 *Teacher Talk*. Garden City, New York: Doubleday.

FUNK AND WAGNALLS

1965 *Standard Dictionary of the English Language* (international edition). Two volumes. New York: Funk and Wagnalls.

GALL, M. D.

1970 "The use of questions in teaching". *Review of Educational Research* 40 (5): 707-21.

GALLO, P.

1966 "Effects of increased incentives upon the use of threats in bargaining". *Journal of Personality and Social Psychology* 4: 14-21.

GEER, B.

1968 "Teaching". Pp. 560-5 in D. L. Shils (ed.), *International Encyclopedia of the Social Sciences*. New York: Macmillan and Free Press.

GERGEN, K. J.

1969 *The Psychology of Behavior Exchange*. Reading, Massachusetts: Addison-Wesley.

GERTH. H., and C. W. MILLS.

1953 *Character and Social Structure*. New York: Harcourt, Brace and World.

GLASER, B. G., and A. L. STRAUSS.

1967 *The Discovery of Grounded Theory: Strategies for Qualitative Research*. Chicago: Aldine.

GOFFMAN, E.

1959 *Presentation of Self and Everyday Life*. Garden City, New York: Doubleday Anchor.

1961 *Encounters: Two Studies in the Sociology of Interaction*. Indianapolis, Indiana: Bobbs-Merrill.

1967 *Interaction Ritual: Essays on Face-to-Face Behavior*. Garden City, New York: Doubleday Anchor.

1970 *Strategic Interaction*. Oxford: Blackwell.

GOSS, J.

1965 "Teaching in the big room". *The National Elementary Principal* 44 (3): 79-82.

GROSS, N., W. S. MASON, and A. W. MC EACHERN.
1958   *Explorations in Role Analysis: Studies of the School Superintendency.* New York: Wiley.

HALL, E. T.
1959   *The Silent Language.* Garden City, New York: Doubleday Anchor.
1969   *The Hidden Dimensions.* Garden City, New York: Doubleday Anchor.

HALL, P. M.
1972   "A symbolic interactionist analysis of politics". Pp. 35-75 in A. Effrat (ed.), *Perspectives in Political Sociology.* Indianapolis: Bobbs-Merrill.

HARE, A. P.
1964   "Interpersonal relations in the small group". Pp. 217-21 in R. E. L. Faris (ed.), *Handbook of Modern Sociology.* Chicago: Rand McNally.

HARGREAVES, D. H.
1967   *Social Relations in a Secondary School.* London: Routledge & Kegan Paul.

HOMANS, G.
1958   "Human behavior as exchange". *American Journal of Sociology* 63 (May): 597-606.
1961   *Social Behavior: Its Elementary Forms.* New York: Harcourt, Brace and World.
1964   "Contemporary theory in sociology". Pp. 951-77 in R. E. L. Faris (ed.), *Handbook of Modern Sociology.* Chicago: Rand McNally.

HOYLE, E.
1969   *The Role of the Teacher.* London: Routledge & Kegan Paul.

HUGHES, M. M.
1963   "Utah study of assessment of teaching". Pp. 25-36 in A. A. Bellack (ed.), *Theory and Research in Teaching.* New York: Bureau of Publications, Teachers College, Columbia University.

INGALLS, E. M.
1969   "So you're teaching in an open area". *The Manitoba Teacher* 48 (1): 4-6.

JACKSON, P.
1968   *Life in Classrooms.* New York: Holt, Rinehart and Winston.

JONES, E. E.
1964   *Ingratiation: a Social Psychological Analysis.* New York: Appleton-Century-Crofts.

LINDESMITH, A. R., and A. L. STRAUSS.
1968   *Social Psychology* (3rd edition). New York: Holt, Rinehart and Winston.

LIPPITT, R., and R. K. WHITE.
1943   "The social climate of children's groups". Pp. 458-508 in R. G. Barker, J. S. Kounin, and H. F. Wright (eds.), *Child Behaviour and Development*. New York: McGraw-Hill.

LORTIE, D. C.
1964   "The teacher and team teaching: suggestions for long-range research". Pp. 270-305 in J. T. Shaplin and H. F. Olds (eds.), *Team Teaching*. New York: Harper and Row.

MARTIN, W. B. W.
1970a   "Preservation of self-esteem: a study in role distance". Unpublished Master of Arts dissertation, Memorial University of Newfoundland, St. John's, Newfoundland.
1970b   "Disparities in urban schools". Pp. 1-23 in Canadian Teachers' Federation (eds.), *The Poor at School in Canada*. Ottawa: Canadian Teachers' Federation.

MC CALL, G. J., and J. L. SIMMONS.
1966   *Identities and Interactions: an Examination of Human Associations in Everyday Life*. New York: Free Press.

MC GRATH, J. E.
1966   "A social psychological approach to the study of negotiations". Pp. 101-34 in R. V. Bowers (ed.), *Studies on Behavior in Organizations*. Athens, Georgia: University of Georgia Press.

MC NUTT, M.
1969   "Open space: room to grow in". *Arbos* 5 (May/June): 4-8.

MEAD, G. H.
1934   *Mind, Self and Society*. (Edited and with introduction by Charles W. Morris.) Chicago: University of Chicago Press.
1936   "The problem of society—how we become selves". Pp. 360-2 in G. H. Mead, *Movements of Thought in the Nineteenth Century*. Chicago: University of Chicago Press.

MEDLEY, D. M., and H. E. MITZEL.
1958   "A technique for measuring classroom behavior". *Journal of Educational Psychology* 49 (April): 86-92.
1963   "Measuring classroom behavior by systematic observation". Pp. 247-328 in N. L. Gage (ed.), *Handbook of Research on Teaching*. Chicago: Rand McNally.

MERTON, R.
1957   *Social Theory and Social Structure* (revised edition). New York: Free Press.
1967   *On Theoretical Sociology*. New York: Free Press.

MILLER, S.
1970   *Prescription for Leadership.* Chicago: Aldine.

MILLS, T. M.
1964   *Group Transformation: an Analysis of a Learning Group.* Englewood Cliffs, New Jersey: Prentice-Hall.

MOYER, J. R.
1965   "An exploratory study of questioning in the instructional processes in selected elementary schools" (doctoral dissertation, Columbia University). Ann Arbor, Michigan: University Microfilms Number 66-2661.

NEWMAN, D. J.
1966   *Conviction: the Determination of Guilt or Innocence without Trial.* Boston, Massachusetts: Little, Brown.

NORD, W. R.
1969   "Social exchange theory: an integrative approach to social conformity". *Psychological Bulletin* 71: 174-208.

OESER, O. A.
1955   *Teacher, Pupil and Task.* London: Tavistock.

OLSEN, M. E.
1968   *The Process of Social Organization.* New York: Holt, Rinehart and Winston.

PARSONS, T.
1951   *The Social System.* New York: Free Press.

PERKINS, H. V.
1951   "Climate influences group learning". *Journal of Educational Research* 45 (October): 115-19.

ROBERTS, J. I.
1971   *Scene of the Battle: Group Behavior in Urban Classrooms.* Garden City, New York: Doubleday Anchor.

ROSE, A. (ed.).
1962   *Human Behavior and Social Processes.* Boston, Massachusetts: Houghton Mifflin.

ROTH, J.
1962   "The treatment of tuberculosis as a bargaining process". Pp. 575-88 in A. Rose (ed.), *Human Behavior and Social Processes.* Boston: Houghton Mifflin.

1963   *Timetables: Structuring the Passage of Time in Hospital Treatment and Other Careers.* Indianapolis, Indiana: Bobbs-Merrill.

SCHATZMAN, L., and R. BUCHER.
1964   "Negotiating a division of labor among professionals in the State Mental Hospital". *Psychiatry* 27 (3): 266-77.

SCHEFF, T. J.
1967   "Toward a sociological model of consensus". *American Sociological Review* 32 (1): 32-46.

1968 "Negotiating reality: notes on power in the assessment of responsibility". *Social Problems* 16 (Summer): 3-17.

SCHELLING, T. C.

1960 *The Strategy of Conflict.* London: Oxford University Press.

SCHRAG, C.

1967 "Elements of theoretical analysis in sociology". Pp. 220-53 in L. Gross, *Sociological Theories: Inquiries and Paradigms.* New York: Harper and Row.

SCHREIBER, J. E.

1967 "Teachers' question-asking techniques in social studies" (doctoral dissertation, University of Iowa). Ann Arbor, Michigan: University Microfilms Number 67-9099.

SHAPLIN, J. T., and H. F. OLDS (eds.).

1964 *Team Teaching.* New York: Harper and Row.

SHIBUTANI, T.

1961 *Society and Personality.* Englewood Cliffs, New Jersey: Prentice-Hall.

SINGLEMANN, P.

1972 "Exchange and symbolic interaction: convergences between two theoretical perspectives". *American Sociological Review* 37 (4): 414-24.

SLATER, P. E.

1966 *Microcosm: Structural, Psychological, and Religious Evolution in Groups.* New York: Wiley.

SMITH, L. M., and J. A. M. BROCK.

1970 *"Go, Bug Go!" Methodological Issues in Classroom Observational Research.* Occasional Papers Series Number 5. St. Ann, Missouri: Central Midwestern Regional Educational Laboratory.

SMITH, L. M., and W. GEOFFREY.

1968 *Complexities of an Urban Classroom.* New York: Holt, Rinehart and Winston.

SMITH, L. M., and P. F. KLEINE.

1969 *Minor Studies in Teacher-Pupil Relationships.* Technical Report Series Number 5. St. Ann, Missouri: Central Midwestern Regional Educational Laboratory.

SOMMER, R.

1969 *Personal Space: the Behavioral Basis of Design.* Englewood Cliffs, New Jersey: Prentice-Hall.

STEBBINS, R. A.

1967 "A theory of the definition of the situation". *Canadian Review of Sociology and Anthropology* 4 (4): 148-64.

1969 "Studying the definition of the situation: theory and field research strategies". *Canadian Review of Sociology and Anthropology* 6 (4): 193-211.

1971 "The meaning of disorderly behavior: teacher definition of a classroom situation". *Sociology of Education* 44 (2): 217-36.

STONE, G. P., and H. A. FARBERMAN (eds.).

1970 *Social Psychology Through Symbolic Interaction.* Waltham, Massachusetts: Xerox College.

STRAUSS, A.

1959 *Mirrors and Masks: the Search for Identity.* Glencoe, Illinois: Free Press.

STRAUSS, A. L., *et al.*

1963 "The hospital and its negotiated order". Pp. 147-69 in E. Freidson (ed.). *The Hospital in Modern Society.* New York: Free Press.

1964 *Psychiatric Ideologies and Institutions.* New York: Free Press.

TRUMP, J. L., and D. BAYNHAN.

1963 *Guide to Better Schools: Focus on Change.* New York: Rand McNally.

TURNER, R. H.

1962 "Role-taking: process versus conformity". Pp. 20-40 in A. Rose (ed.), *Human Behavior and Social Processes.* Boston, Massachusetts: Houghton Mifflin.

WALLER, W.

1932 *The Sociology of Teaching.* New York: Wiley.

WEINSTEIN, E. A., and P. DEUTSCHBERGER.

1964 "Tasks, bargains and identities in social exchange". *Social Forces* 42 (May): 451-6.

WILSON, F. S., R. LANGEVIN, and T. STUCKEY.

1969 *Are Pupils in the Open Plan School Different?* Ottawa: Canadian Council for Research in Education.

WITHALL, J.

1949 "The development of a technique for the measurement of social-emotional climate in classroom". *Journal of Experimental Education* 17 (March), 347-61.

WRONG, D. H.

1969 "Some problems in defining social power". Pp. 46-60 in H. P. Dreitzel (ed.), *Recent Sociology* 1. London: Macmillan.

ZETTERBERG, H.

1965 *On Theory and Verification in Sociology* (3rd edition). Totawa, New Jersey: Bedminster Press.

Index